The Land of Promise

A Comedy in Four Acts

W. Somerset Maugham

Alpha Editions

This edition published in 2022

ISBN : 9789356702134

Design and Setting By
Alpha Editions
www.alphaedis.com
Email - info@alphaedis.com

As per information held with us this book is in Public Domain.
This book is a reproduction of an important historical work. Alpha Editions uses the
best technology to reproduce historical work in the same manner it was first
published to preserve its original nature. Any marks or number seen are left
intentionally to preserve its true form.

ACT I

SCENE: *The drawing-room at Miss Wickham's house in Tunbridge Wells. It is a room in which there is too much furniture. There are armchairs covered with faded chintz, little tables here and there, cabinets containing china, a great many photographs in silver frames, porcelain ornaments wherever there is a vacant space, Chippendale chairs and chairs from the Tottenham Court Road. There are flowers in vases and growing plants. The wall-paper has a pattern of enormous chrysanthemums, and on the walls are a large number of old-fashioned watercolours in gilt frames. There is one door, which leads into the hall; and a French window opens on to the garden. The window is decorated with white lace curtains. It is four o'clock in the afternoon. The sun is streaming through the drawn blinds. There is a wreath of white flowers in a cardboard box on one of the chairs. The door is opened by* KATE, *the parlour-maid. She is of respectable appearance and of a decent age. She admits* MISS PRINGLE. MISS PRINGLE *is companion to a wealthy old lady in Tunbridge Wells. She is a woman of middle age, plainly dressed, thin and narrow of shoulders, with a weather-beaten, tired face and grey hair.*

KATE.

I'll tell Miss Marsh you're here, Miss Pringle.

MISS PRINGLE.

How is she to-day, Kate?

KATE.

She's tired out, poor thing. She's lying down now. But I'm sure she'd like to see you, Miss.

MISS PRINGLE.

I'm very glad she didn't go to the funeral.

KATE.

Dr. Evans thought she'd better stay at home, Miss, and Mrs. Wickham said she'd only upset herself if she went.

MISS PRINGLE.

I wonder how she stood it all those months, waiting on Miss Wickham hand and foot.

KATE.

Miss Wickham wouldn't have a professional nurse. And you know what she was, Miss.... Miss Marsh slept in Miss Wickham's room, and the moment she fell asleep Miss Wickham would have her up because her pillow wanted shaking, or she was thirsty, or something.

MISS PRINGLE.

I suppose she was very inconsiderate.

KATE.

Inconsiderate isn't the word, Miss. I wouldn't be a lady's companion, not for anything. What they have to put up with!

MISS PRINGLE.

Oh, well, everyone isn't like Miss Wickham. The lady I'm companion to, Mrs. Hubbard, is kindness itself.

KATE.

That sounds like Miss Marsh coming downstairs [*She goes to the door and opens it.*] Miss Pringle is here, Miss.

[NORAH *comes in. She is a woman of twenty-eight, with a pleasant, honest face and a happy smile. She is gentle, with quiet manners, but she has a quick temper, under very good control, and a passionate nature which is hidden under a demure appearance. She is simply dressed in black.*]

NORAH.

I *am* glad to see you. I was hoping you'd be able to come here this afternoon.

MISS PRINGLE.

Mrs. Hubbard has gone for a drive with somebody or other, and didn't want me.

[*They kiss one another.* NORAH *notices the wreath.*]

NORAH.

What's this?

KATE.

It didn't arrive till after they'd started, Miss.

NORAH.

I wonder whom it's from. [*She looks at a card which is attached to the wreath.*] "From Mrs. Alfred Vincent, with deepest regret for my dear Miss Wickham and heartiest sympathy for her sorrowing relatives."

KATE.

- 2 -

Sorrowing relatives is good, Miss.

NORAH.

[*Remonstrating.*] Kate ... I think you'd better take it away.

KATE.

What shall I do with it, Miss?

NORAH.

I'm going to the cemetery a little later. I'll take it with me.

KATE.

Very good, Miss.

[KATE *takes up the box and goes out.*]

MISS PRINGLE.

You haven't been crying, Norah?

NORAH.

[*With a little apologetic smile.*] Yes, I couldn't help it.

MISS PRINGLE.

What on earth for?

NORAH.

My dear, it's not unnatural.

MISS PRINGLE.

Well, I don't want to say anything against her now she's dead and gone, poor thing, but Miss Wickham was the most detestable old woman I ever met.

NORAH.

I don't suppose one can live all that time with anyone and not be a little sorry to part with them for ever. I was Miss Wickham's companion for ten years.

MISS PRINGLE.

How you stood it! Exacting, domineering, disagreeable.

NORAH.

Yes, I suppose she was. Because she paid me a salary she thought I wasn't a human being. I never saw anyone with such a bitter tongue. At

- 3 -

first I used to cry every night when I went to bed because of the things she said to me. But I got used to them.

MISS PRINGLE.

I wonder you didn't leave her. I would have.

NORAH.

It's not easy to get posts as lady's companion.

MISS PRINGLE.

That's true. They tell me the agents' books are full of people wanting situations. Before I went to Mrs. Hubbard I was out of one for nearly two years.

NORAH.

It's not so bad for you. You can always go and stay with your brother.

MISS PRINGLE.

You've got a brother too.

NORAH.

Yes, but he's farming in Canada. He had all he could do to keep himself, he couldn't keep me too.

MISS PRINGLE.

How is he doing now?

NORAH.

Oh, he's doing very well. He's got a farm of his own. He wrote over a couple of years ago and told me he could always give me a home if I wanted one.

MISS PRINGLE.

Canada's so far off.

NORAH.

Not when you get there.

MISS PRINGLE.

Why don't you draw the blinds?

NORAH.

I thought I ought to wait till they come back from the funeral.

MISS PRINGLE.

It must be a great relief to you now it's all over.

NORAH.

Sometimes I can't realise it. These last few weeks I hardly got to bed at all, and when the end came I was utterly exhausted. For two days I could do nothing but sleep. Poor Miss Wickham. She did hate dying.

MISS PRINGLE.

That's the extraordinary part of it. I believe you were really fond of her.

NORAH.

D'you know that for nearly a year she would eat nothing but what I gave her with my own hands. And she liked me as much as she was capable of liking anybody.

MISS PRINGLE.

That wasn't much.

NORAH.

And then, I was so dreadfully sorry for her.

MISS PRINGLE.

Good heavens!

NORAH.

She'd been a hard and selfish woman all her life, and there was no one who cared for her. It seemed so dreadful to die like that and leave not a soul to regret one. Her nephew and his wife were just waiting for her death. It was dreadful. Each time they came down from London I saw them looking at her to see if she was any worse than when last they'd seen her.

MISS PRINGLE.

Well, I thought her a horrid old woman, and I'm glad she's dead. And I hope she's left you well provided for.

NORAH.

[*With a smile.*] Oh, I think she's done that. Two years ago when I nearly went away she said she'd left me enough to live upon.

MISS PRINGLE.

You mean when that assistant of Dr. Evans wanted to marry you? I'm glad you wouldn't have him.

NORAH.

He was very nice. But, of course, he wasn't a gentleman.

MISS PRINGLE.

I shouldn't like to live with a man at all; I think they're horrid, but, of course, it would be impossible if he weren't a gentleman.

NORAH.

[*With a twinkle in her eye.*] He came to see Miss Wickham, but she wouldn't have anything to do with him. First she said that she couldn't spare me, and then she said that I had a very bad temper.

MISS PRINGLE.

I like *her* saying that.

NORAH.

It's quite true. Every now and then I felt I couldn't put up with her any more. I forgot that I was dependent on her, and if she dismissed me I probably shouldn't be able to find another situation, and I just flew at her. I must say she was very nice about it; she used to look at me and grin, and, when it was all over, say: "My dear, when you marry, if your husband's a wise man, he'll use a big stick now and then."

MISS PRINGLE.

Old cat.

NORAH.

[*Smiling.*] I should like to see a man try.

MISS PRINGLE.

How much d'you think she's left you?

NORAH.

Well, of course, I don't know; the will is going to be read this afternoon when they come back from the funeral, but from what she said I believe about two hundred and fifty a year.

MISS PRINGLE.

It's the least she could do. She's had the ten best years of your life.

NORAH.

[*With a sigh of relief.*] I shall never be at anybody's beck and call again. I shall be able to get up when I like and go to bed when I like, go out when I choose, and come in when I choose.

MISS PRINGLE.

[*Drily.*] You'll probably marry.

NORAH.

Never.

MISS PRINGLE.

Then what'll you do?

NORAH.

I shall go to Italy, Florence, Rome. D'you think it's horrible of me, I'm so happy?

MISS PRINGLE.

My dear child.

[*There is a sound of carriage wheels on the drive.*]

NORAH.

There they are.

MISS PRINGLE.

I'd better go, hadn't I?

NORAH.

I'm afraid you must.

MISS PRINGLE.

I do so want to know about the will. Can't I go up to your room and wait there?

NORAH.

No. I'll tell you what, go and sit in the garden. They want to catch the four something back to London, and we can have a cosy little tea all by ourselves.

MISS PRINGLE.

Very well. Oh, my dear, I'm so happy in your good luck.

NORAH.

Take care.

[MISS PRINGLE *slips out into the garden, and a moment later* MR. *and* MRS. WICKHAM *enter the room.* MRS. WICKHAM *is a pretty young woman. She is dressed in black, but her gown is elegant and fashionable.* JAMES WICKHAM *is a clean-shaven, thin-faced man, with a baldish head. He is dressed in black and wears black kid gloves.*]

DOROTHY.

[*Cheerfully.*] Ouf! Do put the blinds up, Miss Marsh. We really needn't be depressed any more. Jim, if you love me, take those gloves off. They're perfectly revolting.

[NORAH *goes to the window and draws up the blind.*]

WICKHAM.

Why, what's wrong with them? The fellow in the shop told me they were the right thing.

DOROTHY.

I never saw anyone look quite so funereal as you do.

WICKHAM.

Well, you didn't want me to get myself up as though I were going to a wedding, did you?

NORAH.

Were there many people?

DOROTHY.

Quite a lot. The sort of people who indulge in other people's funerals as a mild form of dissipation.

WICKHAM.

[*Looking at his watch.*] I hope Wynne will look sharp. I don't want to miss that train.

DOROTHY.

Who were all those stodgy old things who wrung your hand afterwards, Jim?

WICKHAM.

I can't think. They made me feel such a fool.

DOROTHY.

Oh, was that it? I saw you looking a perfect owl, and I thought you were giving a very bad imitation of restrained emotion.

WICKHAM.

[*Remonstrating.*] Dorothy.

NORAH.

Would you like some tea, Mrs. Wickham?

DOROTHY.

Well, you might send some in so that it'll be ready when Mr. Wynne comes.

[NORAH *is just going to ring the bell, but* MRS. WICKHAM *stops her with a pleasant smile.*]

We'll ring for you, shall we? I daresay you've got one or two things you want to do now.

NORAH.

Very good, Mrs. Wickham.

[*She goes out.*]

WICKHAM.

I say, Dorothy, you oughtn't to be facetious before Miss Marsh. She was extremely attached to Aunt Louisa.

DOROTHY.

Oh, what nonsense! It's always a very good rule to judge people by oneself, and I'm positive she was just longing for the old lady to die.

WICKHAM.

She was awfully upset at the end.

DOROTHY.

Nerves! Men are so idiotic. They never understand that there are tears *and* tears. I cried myself, and heaven knows I didn't regret her death.

WICKHAM.

My dear Dorothy, you oughtn't to say that.

DOROTHY.

Why not? It's perfectly true. Aunt Louisa was a detestable person and no one would have stood her for a minute if she hadn't had money. I don't see any use in being a hypocrite now that it can't make any difference either way.

WICKHAM.

[*Looking at his watch again.*] I wish Wynne would hurry up. It'll be beastly inconvenient if we miss that train.

DOROTHY.

I don't trust Miss Marsh. She looks as if she knew what was in the will.

WICKHAM.

I don't suppose she does. Aunt Louisa wasn't the sort of person to talk.

DOROTHY.

I'm sure she knows she's been left something.

WICKHAM.

Oh, well, I think she has a right to expect that. Aunt Louisa led her a dog's life.

DOROTHY.

She had wages and a comfortable home. If she didn't like the place she could have left it.... After all it's family money. I don't think Aunt Louisa had the right to leave it to strangers.

WICKHAM.

We oughtn't to complain if Miss Marsh gets a small annuity. Aunt Louisa promised her something of the sort when she had a chance of marrying a couple of years ago.

DOROTHY.

Miss Marsh is quite young. It isn't as if she'd been here for thirty years.

WICKHAM.

Well, I've got an idea that Aunt Louisa meant to leave her about two hundred and fifty a year.

DOROTHY.

But what's the estate?

WICKHAM.

About nineteen thousand pounds, I believe.

DOROTHY.

Oh, it's absurd. It's a most unfair proportion. It makes all the difference to us. On that extra two hundred and fifty a year we could almost keep a car.

WICKHAM.

My dear, be thankful if we get anything at all.

DOROTHY.

[*Aghast.*] Jim! [*She stares at him.*] Jim, you don't think! Oh! That would be too horrible.

WICKHAM.

Take care.

[*The door opens and* KATE *brings in the tea-things. She puts them on a small table.*]

How lucky it is we had a fine day, isn't it?

DOROTHY.

Yes.

WICKHAM.

It looks as if we were going to have a spell of fine weather.

DOROTHY.

Yes.

WICKHAM.

It's funny how often it rains for weddings.

DOROTHY.

Very funny.

[*Exit* KATE.]

I've been counting on that money for years. I used to dream at night that I was reading a telegram with the news of Aunt Louisa's death. And I've thought of all we should be able to do when we got it. It'll make such a difference.

WICKHAM.

You know what she was. She didn't care two-pence for us. We ought to be prepared for the worst.

DOROTHY.

D'you think she could have left everything to Miss Marsh?

WICKHAM.

I shouldn't be surprised.

DOROTHY.

We'll dispute the will. It's undue influence. I suspected Miss Marsh from the beginning. I hate her. Oh, why doesn't Wynne come?

[*There is a ring at the bell.*]

WICKHAM.

Here he is, I expect.

DOROTHY.

The suspense is too awful.

WICKHAM.

Pull yourself together, old girl. And I say, look a bit dismal. After all, we've just come from a funeral.

DOROTHY.

Are we downhearted?

[KATE *enters to announce* MR. WYNNE.]

KATE.

Mr. Wynne.

[*He enters and she goes out and closes the door.* MR. WYNNE, *the late Miss Wickham's solicitor, is a tallish man with a bald head. He has the red cheeks and hearty manner of a man who plays in his spare time at being a country gentleman. He is dressed in mourning because he has been to Miss Wickham's funeral.*]

WICKHAM.

Hulloa!

WYNNE.

[*Taking* DOROTHY'S *hand rather solemnly.*] I didn't have an opportunity of shaking hands with you at the cemetery.

DOROTHY.

[*Somewhat helplessly.*] How do you do?

- 12 -

WYNNE.

Pray accept my sincerest sympathy on your great bereavement.

DOROTHY.

Of course, the end was not entirely unexpected.

WYNNE.

No, I know. But it must have been a great shock all the same.

WICKHAM.

My wife was very much upset, but of course my poor aunt had suffered great pain, and we couldn't help looking upon it as a happy release.

WYNNE.

How is Miss Marsh?

[DOROTHY *gives him a quick look, wondering whether there is anything behind the polite inquiry.*]

DOROTHY.

Oh, she's very well.

WYNNE.

Her devotion to Miss Wickham was wonderful. Dr. Evans—he's my brother-in-law, you know—told me no trained nurse could have been more competent. She was like a daughter to Miss Wickham.

DOROTHY.

[*Rather coldly.*] I suppose we'd better send for her.

WICKHAM.

Have you brought the.... [*He stops in some embarrassment.*]

WYNNE.

Yes, I have it in my pocket.

DOROTHY.

I'll ring.

[*She touches the bell.*]

WICKHAM.

I expect Mr. Wynne would like a cup of tea, Dorothy.

DOROTHY.

Oh, I'm so sorry, I quite forgot about it.

WYNNE.

No, thank you very much. I never take tea.

[*He takes a long envelope out of his pocket, and from it the will. He smooths it out reflectively.* DOROTHY *gives the document a nervous glance.* KATE *comes in.*]

WICKHAM.

Will you ask Miss Marsh to be good enough to come here.

KATE.

Very good, sir.

[*Exit.*]

DOROTHY.

What is the time, Jim?

WICKHAM.

[*Looking at his watch.*] Oh, there's no hurry. [*To* WYNNE.] We've got an important engagement in London this evening. We're very anxious not to miss the fast train.

DOROTHY.

The train service is rotten.

WYNNE.

The will is very short. It won't take me two minutes to read it.

DOROTHY.

[*Nervous and impatient.*] What on earth is Miss Marsh doing?

WYNNE.

How pretty the garden is looking now.

WICKHAM.

[*Abruptly.*] Very.

WYNNE.

Miss Wickham was always so interested in her garden.

DOROTHY.

Yes.

WYNNE.

My own tulips aren't so advanced as those.

WICKHAM.

[*Irritably.*] Aren't they?

WYNNE.

[*To* DOROTHY.] Are you interested in gardening?

DOROTHY.

[*Hardly able to control her impatience.*] No, I hate it.... At last!

[*The door is opened and* MISS MARSH *comes in.* WYNNE *gets up.*]

WYNNE.

How d'you do, Miss Marsh?

NORAH.

How d'you do?

WICKHAM.

Will you have a cup of tea?

DOROTHY.

[*All nerves.*] Jim, Miss Marsh would much prefer to have tea quietly after we're gone.

NORAH.

[*With a faint smile.*] I won't have any tea, thank you.

DOROTHY.

Mr. Wynne has brought the will with him.

NORAH.

Oh, yes.

[*She sits down calmly.* DOROTHY, *with clenched hands, watches her. She tries to make out from her face whether* NORAH *knows anything.*]

WYNNE.

Miss Marsh, so far as you know, there's no other will?

NORAH.

How d'you mean?

WYNNE.

Miss Wickham didn't make a later one—without my assistance, I mean? You know of nothing in the house, for instance?

NORAH.

[*Quite decidedly.*] Oh, no. Miss Wickham always said you had her will. She was extremely methodical.

WYNNE.

I feel I ought to ask because she consulted me about making a fresh will a couple of years ago. She told me what she wanted to do, but gave me no actual instructions to draw it. I thought perhaps she might have done it herself.

NORAH.

I heard nothing about it. I'm sure that her only will is in your hands.

WYNNE.

Then I think we may take it that this....

[DOROTHY *suddenly understands; she interrupts quickly.*]

DOROTHY.

When was that will made?

WYNNE.

Eight or nine years ago.... The exact date was March 4th, 1904.

[DOROTHY *gives Norah a long, searching look.*]

DOROTHY.

When did you first come to Miss Wickham?

NORAH.

At the end of nineteen hundred and three.

[*There is a slight pause.*]

WYNNE.

Shall I read it, or would you just like to know the particulars? It is very short.

DOROTHY.

Let us just know roughly.

WYNNE.

Well, Miss Wickham left one hundred pounds to the Society for the Propagation of the Gospel, and one hundred pounds to the General Hospital at Tunbridge Wells, and the entire residue of her fortune to her nephew, Mr. James Wickham.

[DOROTHY *gives a sharp inspiration of triumph. She looks again at* NORAH, *but* NORAH *gives no sign of emotion.*]

WICKHAM.

And Miss Marsh?

WYNNE.

Miss Marsh is not mentioned.

NORAH.

[*With a faint smile.*] I could hardly expect to be. At the time the will was drawn I had been Miss Wickham's companion for only a few months.

WYNNE.

That is why I asked whether you knew of any later will. When I talked to Miss Wickham on the subject she said her wish was to make adequate provision for you after her death. I think she had spoken to you about it.

NORAH.

Yes.

WYNNE.

She mentioned three hundred a year.

NORAH.

That was very kind of her. I'm glad she wished to do something for me.

WYNNE.

Oddly enough she spoke about it to Dr. Evans only a few days before she died.

WICKHAM.

Perhaps there *is* a later will somewhere?

WYNNE.

I honestly don't think so.

NORAH.

I'm sure there isn't.

WYNNE.

Dr. Evans was talking to Miss Wickham about Miss Marsh. She was tired out and he wanted Miss Wickham to have a professional nurse. She told him then that I had the will and she had left Miss Marsh amply provided for.

DOROTHY.

[*Quickly.*] That isn't legal, of course?

WYNNE.

What isn't?

DOROTHY.

I mean, no one could force us—I mean, the will stands as it is, doesn't it?

WYNNE.

Certainly.

WICKHAM.

I'm afraid it's a great disappointment to you, Miss Marsh.

NORAH.

[*Lightly.*] I never count my chickens before they're hatched.

WYNNE.

It would be very natural if Miss Marsh were disappointed under the circumstances. I think she'd been led to expect....

DOROTHY.

[*Interrupting.*] Our aunt left a very small fortune, I understand, and I suppose she felt it wouldn't be fair to leave a large part of it away from her own family.

WICKHAM.

Of course, it is family money; she inherited it from my grandfather, and ... but I want you to know, Miss Marsh, that my wife and I thoroughly appreciate all you did for my aunt. Money couldn't repay your care and devotion. You've been perfectly wonderful.

NORAH.

It's extremely good of you to say so. I was very fond of Miss Wickham. Nothing I did for her was any trouble.

WYNNE.

I think everyone who saw Miss Marsh with Miss Wickham must be aware that during the ten years she was with her she never spared herself.

WICKHAM.

[*Hesitatingly, with a glance at his wife.*] Of course, my aunt was a very trying woman.

DOROTHY.

[*Agreeably.*] Earning one's living is always unpleasant. If it weren't there'd be no incentive to work.

[NORAH *gives her a glance of quiet amusement at this surprising remark.*]

WICKHAM.

My wife and I would be very glad to make some kind of acknowledgment of your services.

DOROTHY.

I was just going to mention it.

WYNNE.

[*Brightening a little.*] I felt sure that under the circumstances....

DOROTHY.

[*Interrupting him quickly.*] What were your wages, Miss Marsh?

NORAH.

Thirty pounds a year.

DOROTHY.

Really? Many ladies are glad to go as companion without any salary, just for the sake of a home and congenial society. I daresay you've been able to save a good deal in all these years.

NORAH.

[*Frigidly.*] I had to dress myself decently, Mrs. Wickham.

DOROTHY.

[*With all the charm she can put into her manner.*] Well, I'm sure my husband will be very glad to give you a year's salary, won't you, Jim?

NORAH.

It's very kind of you, but I'm not inclined to accept anything but what's legally due to me.

DOROTHY.

[*Undisturbed.*] You must remember that there'll be very heavy death duties to pay. They'll swallow up the income from Miss Wickham's estate for at least two years, won't they, Mr. Wynne?

NORAH.

I quite understand.

DOROTHY.

Perhaps you'll change your mind.

NORAH.

I don't think so.

[*There is a slight, rather awkward pause.* MR. WYNNE *gets up. His manner shows that he is not impressed by* MRS. WICKHAM'S *generosity.*]

WYNNE.

Well, I think I must leave you.

WICKHAM.

We must go, too, Dorothy.

DOROTHY.

[*Quite at ease.*] Oh, it'll only take five minutes to get down to the station in a cab.

WYNNE.

Good-bye, Miss Marsh. If I can be of any help to you I hope you'll let me know.

NORAH.

That's very kind of you.

WYNNE.

[*To* DOROTHY.] Good-bye.

[*He bows slightly to her, nods to* WICKHAM *and during* DOROTHY'S *next speech goes out.*]

DOROTHY.

[*Very friendly and affable.*] Jim will be writing to you in a day or two. You know how grateful we both are for all you did for our poor aunt. We shall be glad to give you the very highest references.

WICKHAM.

[*Relieved to be able to offer something.*] Oh, yes, we'll do everything we can.

DOROTHY.

You're such a wonderful nurse, I'm sure you'll have no difficulty in getting another situation. I expect I can find you something myself. I'll ask among all my friends.

[NORAH *looks at her reflectively, but does not answer.* DOROTHY *beams and smiles at her.*]

WICKHAM.

Come on, Dorothy, we really haven't got any time to lose. Good-bye, Miss Marsh.

NORAH.

Good-bye.

[*They bustle out and in a moment the sound is heard of wheels on the drive as the cab carries them away.* NORAH *is left alone. She stands staring in front of her. She does not hear* MISS PRINGLE *come in from the garden.*]

MISS PRINGLE.

I thought they were never going. Well?

[NORAH *turns and looks at her without a word.*

[MISS PRINGLE *is startled.*] Norah! What's the matter? Isn't it as much as you thought?

NORAH.

Miss Wickham's left me nothing.

MISS PRINGLE.

Oh!

NORAH.

Not a penny! Oh, it's cruel. After all, there was no need for her to leave me anything. She gave me board and lodging and thirty pounds a year. If I stayed it was because I chose. She needn't have promised me anything. She needn't have prevented me from marrying.

MISS PRINGLE.

My dear, you could never have married the little assistant. He wasn't a gentleman.

NORAH.

Ten years! The ten best years of a woman's life, when other girls are enjoying themselves. And what did I get for it? Board and lodging and thirty pounds a year. A cook does better than that.

MISS PRINGLE.

We can't expect to make so much money as a good cook. One has to pay something for living like a lady among people of one's own class.

NORAH.

Oh, it's cruel.

MISS PRINGLE.

[*Trying to console her.*] My dear, don't give way. I'm sure you'll have no difficulty in finding another situation. You wash lace beautifully, and no one can arrange flowers like you.

NORAH.

I was dreaming of France and Italy.... I shall spend ten years more with an old lady, and then she'll die, and I shall look out for another situation. It won't be so easy then because I shan't be so young. And so it'll go on till I can't find a situation because I'm too old, and some charitable people will get me into a home. You like the life, don't you?

MISS PRINGLE.

My dear, there are so few things a gentlewoman can do.

NORAH.

When I think of these ten years! Having to put up with every unreasonableness! Never being allowed to feel ill or tired! No servant would have stood what I have. The humiliation I've endured!

MISS PRINGLE.

You're tired and out of sorts. Everyone isn't so trying as Miss Wickham. I'm sure Mrs. Hubbard has been kindness itself to me.

NORAH.

Considering.

MISS PRINGLE.

I don't know what you mean by considering.

NORAH.

Considering that she's rich and you're poor. She gives you her old clothes. She often doesn't ask you to have dinner by yourself when she's giving a party. She doesn't remind you that you're dependent unless she's very much put out. But you—you've had thirty years of it. You've eaten the bitter bread of slavery till—till it tastes like plum cake.

MISS PRINGLE.

[*Rather hurt.*] I don't know why you say such things to me, Norah.

[*Before* NORAH *has time to answer* KATE *comes in.*]

KATE.

Mr. Hornby would like to see you for a minute, Miss.

NORAH.

[*Surprised.*] Now?

KATE.

I told him I didn't think it would be convenient, Miss, but he says it's very important, and he won't detain you more than five minutes.

NORAH.

What a nuisance.... Ask him to come in.

KATE.

Very good, Miss. [*Exit.*]

NORAH.

I wonder what on earth he wants.

MISS PRINGLE.

Who is he, Norah?

NORAH.

Oh, he's the son of Colonel Hornby. Don't you know, he lives at the top of Molyneux Park. His mother was a great friend of Miss Wickham's. He comes down here now and then for week-ends. He's got something to do with motor-cars.

[KATE *shows the visitor in.*]

KATE.

Mr. Hornby.

[*She goes out.* REGINALD HORNBY *is a good-looking young man, with a neat head on a long, elegant body. His dark, sleek hair is carefully brushed, his small moustache is trim and curled. His beautiful clothes suggest the fashionable tailors of Savile Row. His tie, his handkerchief protruding from the breast pocket, his boots, are the very latest thing. He is a nut.*]

HORNBY.

I say, I'm awfully sorry to blow in like this. But I didn't know if you'd be staying on here, and I wanted to catch you. And I'm off in a day or two, myself.

NORAH.

Won't you sit down? Mr. Hornby—Miss Pringle.

HORNBY.

How d'you do? Everything go off O.K.?

NORAH.

I beg your pardon?

HORNBY.

Funeral, I mean. Mother went. Regular beano for her.

[MISS PRINGLE, *rather shocked, draws herself up primly, but* NORAH'S *eyes twinkle with amusement at his airy manner.*]

NORAH.

Really?

HORNBY.

You see, she's getting on. I'm the child of her old age—Benjamin, don't you know. [*He turns to Miss Pringle.*] Benjamin and Sarah, you know.

MISS PRINGLE.

I understand perfectly, but it wasn't Sarah.

HORNBY.

Wasn't it? When one of her old friends dies, mother goes to the funeral and says to herself: "Well, I've seen her out, anyhow." Then she comes back and eats muffins for tea. She always eats muffins after she's been to a funeral.

NORAH.

The maid said you wanted to see about something.

HORNBY.

That's right, I was forgetting. [*To Miss Pringle.*] If Sarah wasn't Benjamin's mother, whose mother was she?

MISS PRINGLE.

If you want to know, I recommend you to read your Bible.

HORNBY.

[*With much satisfaction.*] I thought it was a stumper. [*To* NORAH.] The fact is, I'm going to Canada, and mother told me you'd got a brother or something out there.

NORAH.

A brother, not a something.

HORNBY.

And she said, perhaps you wouldn't mind giving me a letter to him.

NORAH.

I will with pleasure. But I'm afraid he won't be much use to you. He's a farmer and he lives miles away from anywhere.

HORNBY.

But I'm going in for farming.

NORAH.

Are you? What on earth for?

HORNBY.

I've jolly well got to do something, and I think farming's about the best thing I can do. One gets a lot of shooting and riding, you know. And then there are tennis parties and dances. And you make a pot of money, there's no doubt about that.

NORAH.

I thought you were in some motor business in London.

HORNBY.

Well, I was in a way. But ... I thought you'd have heard about it. Mother's been telling everybody. Governor won't speak to me. Altogether things are rotten. I want to get out of this beastly country as quick as I can.

NORAH.

Would you like me to give you the letter at once?

HORNBY.

I wish you would.

[NORAH *sits down at an escritoire and begins to write a letter.*]

Fact is, I'm broke. I was all right as long as I stuck to bridge. I used to make money on that. Over a thousand a year.

MISS PRINGLE.

[*Horrified.*] What!

HORNBY.

Playing regularly, you know. If I hadn't been a fool I'd have stuck to that. But I got bitten with *chemi*.

NORAH.

[*Turning round.*] With what?

HORNBY.

Chemin de fer. Never heard of it? I got in the habit of going to Thornton's. I suppose you never heard of him either. He keeps a gambling hell. Gives you a slap-up supper for nothing, as much pop as you can drink, and changes your cheques like a bird. The result is I've lost every bob I had, and then Thornton sued me on a cheque I'd given him. The Governor forked out, but he says I've got to go to Canada. I'm never going to gamble again, I can tell you that.

NORAH.

Oh, well, that's something.

HORNBY.

You can't make money at *chemi*. The *cagnotte's* bound to clear you out in the end. When I come back I'm going to stick to bridge. There are always plenty of mugs about, and if you've got a good head for cards you can't help making an income out of it.

NORAH.

Here is your letter.

HORNBY.

Thanks awfully. I daresay I shan't want it, you know. I expect I shall get offered a job the moment I land, but there's no harm having it. I'll be getting along.

NORAH.

Good-bye, then, and good luck.

HORNBY.

Good-bye.

[*He shakes hands with* NORAH *and* MISS PRINGLE *and goes out.*]

MISS PRINGLE.

Norah, why don't *you* go to Canada? Now your brother has a farm of his own I should have thought....

NORAH.

[*Interrupting.*] My brother's married. He married four years ago.

MISS PRINGLE.

You never told me.

NORAH.

I couldn't.

MISS PRINGLE.

Why? Isn't his wife ... isn't his wife nice?

NORAH.

She was a waitress at a scrubby little hotel in Winnipeg.

MISS PRINGLE.

What are you going to do, then?

NORAH.

It's no good crying over spilt milk. I'll look out for another situation.

END OF FIRST ACT

ACT II

SCENE: *The living-room and kitchen on* EDWARD MARSH'S *farm at Dyer, Manitoba. It is a room lined with brown planks, and on the walls in cheap gilt frames are coloured supplements from the Christmas numbers of illustrated papers. Over one door is the head of a moose, and over the other a large kitchen clock. The floor is covered with shiny oil-cloth. In the window are geraniums growing in maple-syrup tins. On one side is a large American stove. There is a dresser of unvarnished deal on which are plates and cups and saucers. They are of the plainest earthenware, and few of them match. There are two American rockers and a number of kitchen chairs. There is a plain kitchen table. On the stove is an enormous kettle and a couple of saucepans. There is a small bookshelf on which are a few tattered novels and some old magazines. The table is set for dinner with a cheap white cloth, none too clean.* ED MARSH *is sitting at one end, with the remains of a joint of cold beef in front of him, and at the other end is his wife, with a teapot, milk-jug, and sugar-basin. There is a loaf of bread on the table, a large tin containing maple-syrup, and the remains of a milk pudding.* NORAH *is sitting next to her sister-in-law and beside her is* REGINALD HORNBY. *Opposite are* FRANK TAYLOR *and* BENJAMIN TROTTER. *Dinner is just finished.* GERTIE MARSH *is a dark little person, with a hard look and a dried-up skin. She is thin and nervous, an active, hard-working woman with a sharp tongue and, outwardly at least, little tenderness. She is dressed in a shirt-waist, a serge skirt, and brown, rather smart high-heeled shoes. She wears a small apron.* NORAH *wears a white blouse and a green skirt.* ED MARSH *is a good-natured, easy-going man, with a small moustache and untidy hair. He wears a black flannel shirt, with white lines on it, a black waistcoat, and dark grubby trousers. The others are hired men.* FRANK TAYLOR *is a tall fellow, strong, with clean-cut features and frank, humorous eyes. He is clean shaven. His movements are slow and he speaks with a marked accent. He is very sure of himself. He wears a dark flannel shirt and a pair of overalls, which have been blue, but are now black and grimy with age. The braces which hold them up announce that they come from Eaton's, Winnipeg.* BEN TROTTER *is an English labourer, with broken, discoloured teeth, and hair cut very short, with something like a love-lock plastered on his forehead. He is dressed in the same way as* FRANK TAYLOR. REGGIE HORNBY'S *head is still neat and trim, his hair is carefully brushed. His overalls are much newer than the others'. He wears a flannel shirt which was obviously made in Piccadilly.*

MARSH.

Have some more syrup, Reg?

HORNBY.

No, thank you.

MARSH.

Has everyone finished?

GERTIE.

It looks like it.

[MARSH *pushes back his chair, takes a pouch and pipe from his pocket and lights up.* TAYLOR *does the same.*]

GERTIE.

We'll be able to start on the ironing this afternoon.

NORAH.

Very well.

TROTTER.

It was a rare big wash you done this morning by the look of it on the line.

NORAH.

My arms are just aching.

GERTIE.

When you've been out in this country a bit longer you'll learn not to wear more things than you can help.

NORAH.

Was there more than my fair share?

GERTIE.

You use double the number of stockings than what I do. And everything else is the same.

NORAH.

[*With a smile.*] Clean but incompetent.

GERTIE.

There's many a true word spoken in jest.

TAYLOR.

Say, Reg, is it true that when you first come out you asked Ed where the bath-room was?

TROTTER.

[*With a chuckle.*] That's right. Ed told 'im there was a river a mile and a 'alf from 'ere, an' that was the only bath-room 'e knew.

MARSH.

One soon gets used to that sort of thing, eh, Reg?

HORNBY.

Rather. If I saw a bath-room now it would only make me nervous.

TAYLOR.

Out in B.C. I knew a couple of Englishmen who were baching and the only other people around were Indians. The first two years they was there they wouldn't have anything to do with the Indians because they was so dirty, and after that the Indians wouldn't have anything to do with them. [*He puts his fingers to his nose to indicate a nasty smell.*]

NORAH.

What a disgusting story!

TAYLOR.

D'you think so? I rather like it.

NORAH.

You would.

[*He looks at her with a little smile, but does not answer.*]

GERTIE.

[*Getting up.*] Are you going to sit there all day, Norah?

MARSH.

Why don't you keep quiet for five minutes? I guess Norah's not sorry to have a rest after that wash.

GERTIE.

The amount of work Norah did isn't going to tire her much, I reckon.

NORAH.

I'm not used to that sort of work yet. It takes it out of me a bit.

GERTIE.

I've not found out what sort of work you are used to.

[NORAH *gets up and the two women start clearing away the table.* MARSH *moves into one of the rocking-chairs and smokes.*]

MARSH.

Give her time to get used to the life, Gertie. You can't expect everything all at once.

GERTIE.

It's always the same with English people. You have to teach them everything.

MARSH.

Well, you didn't have to teach me to propose, Gertie.

[NORAH *takes away things from before* TAYLOR *and he gets up.*]

TAYLOR.

I guess I'm in your way.

NORAH.

Not more than usual, thank you.

TAYLOR.

[*Smiling.*] I guess you'll not be sorry to see the last of me.

NORAH.

I can't honestly say that it makes the least difference to me whether you go or stay.

MARSH.

Now don't start quarrelling, you two.

HORNBY.

When does your train go, Frank?

TAYLOR.

Half-past three. I'll be starting from here in about an hour.

MARSH.

Reg can go over with you and he'll drive the rig back again.

TAYLOR.

All right. I'll go and dress myself in a bit.

GERTIE.

I guess you'll be glad to get back to your own place.

TAYLOR.

I guess I shan't be sorry.

[*The clearing away is finished.* GERTIE *gets a large metal basin and puts it on the table.* NORAH *fetches the kettle and pours hot water into the basin. They begin washing up.*]

GERTIE.

I'll do the washing, Norah, and you can dry.

NORAH.

All right.

GERTIE.

I've noticed the things aren't half clean when I leave them to you to do.

NORAH.

I'm sorry. Why didn't you tell me?

GERTIE.

I suppose *you* never did the washing up in England. Too grand?

NORAH.

I don't suppose anyone would wash up if they could help it. It's not very amusing.

GERTIE.

You always want to be amused.

NORAH.

No. But I want to be happy.

GERTIE.

Well, you've got a room over your head and a comfortable bed to sleep in, three good meals a day, and plenty to do; that's all anybody wants to make them happy, I guess.

HORNBY.

Oh, lord!

GERTIE.

[*Turning sharply on him.*] Well, if you don't like Canada, why did you come out?

- 32 -

HORNBY.

[*Rising slowly to his feet.*] You don't suppose I'd have let them send me if I'd known what I was in for? Not much. Up at five in the morning and working in the fields like a navvy till your back feels as if it 'ud break, and then back again in the afternoon. And the same thing day after day. What was the good of sending me to Harrow and Oxford if that's what I've got to do all my life?

MARSH.

You'll get used to it soon enough, Reg. It's a bit hard at first, but when you get your foot in you wouldn't change it for any other life.

GERTIE.

This isn't a country for a man to go to sleep with and wait for something to turn up.

TROTTER.

I wouldn't go back to England now, not for nothing. England! Eighteen bob a week, that's what I earned, and no prospects. Out of work five months in the year.

NORAH.

What did you do in England?

TROTTER.

Bricklayer, Miss.

GERTIE.

You needn't call her miss. Norah's her name. You call me Gertie, don't you?

TROTTER.

What with strikes an' bad times you never knew where you was. And the foreman bullying you. I don't know what all. I 'ad about enough of it, I can tell you. I've never been out of work since the day I landed. I've had as much to eat as I wanted and I'm saving money. In this country everybody's as good as everybody else.

NORAH.

If not better.

TROTTER.

In two years I shall be able to set up for myself. Why, there's old man Thompson, up at Pratt, he started as a bricklayer, come from Yorkshire, he did. He's got seven thousand dollars in the bank now.

MARSH.

You fellows who come out now have a much softer thing on than I did when I first came. In those days they wouldn't have an Englishman, they'd have a Galician rather. In Winnipeg, when they advertised in the paper for labour, you'd see often as not no English need apply.

GERTIE.

Well, it was their own fault. They wouldn't work or anything. They just soaked.

MARSH.

It was their own fault right enough. This was the dumping ground for all the idlers, drunkards, and scallywags in England. They had the delusion over there that if a man was too big a rotter to do anything at all in England he'd only got to be sent out here and he'd make a fortune.

TAYLOR.

I guess things ain't as bad as that now. They send us a different class. It takes an Englishman two years longer than anybody else to get the hang of things, but when once he tumbles to it he's better than any of them.

MARSH.

I guess nowadays everyone's glad to see the Englishman make good. When I nearly smashed up three years ago, I had no end of offers to help.

HORNBY.

How did you smash up?

MARSH.

Oh, I had a run of bad luck. One year my crop was frosted and then next year I was hailed out. It wants a good deal of capital to stand up against that.

TAYLOR.

That's what happened to me. I was hailed out, and I hadn't got capital, so I just had to hire out. [*To* NORAH.] If it hadn't been for that hailstorm you wouldn't have had the pleasure of making my acquaintance.

NORAH.

[*Ironically.*] How hollow and empty life would have been without that.

GERTIE.

I wonder you didn't just quit and start out Calgary way.

TAYLOR.

Well, I'd put in two years on my homestead and done a lot of clearing. It seemed kind of silly to lose my rights now. And when you've been hailed out once the chances are it won't happen again, for some years that is, and by that time I ought to have put a bit by.

NORAH.

What sort of a house have you got?

TAYLOR.

Well, it ain't what you might call a palace, but it's large enough for two.

MARSH.

Thinking of marrying?

TAYLOR.

Well, I guess it's kind of lonesome on a farm without a woman. But it's not so easy to find a wife when you're just starting on your own. Canadian girls think twice before taking a farmer.

GERTIE.

They know something, I guess.

MARSH.

Well, you took one, Gertie.

GERTIE.

Not because I wanted to, you can be sure of that. I don't know how you got round me.

MARSH.

I wonder.

GERTIE.

I guess it was because you was kind of helpless, and I didn't know what you'd do without me.

MARSH.

I guess it was love and you couldn't help yourself.

TAYLOR.

I'm thinking of going to one of them employment agencies when I get to Winnipeg and looking the girls over.

NORAH.

Like sheep.

TAYLOR.

I don't know anythin' about sheep. I've never had to do with sheep.

NORAH.

And d'you think you know anything about women?

TAYLOR.

I guess I can tell if they're strong and willing. And so long as they ain't cock-eyed I don't mind taking the rest on trust.

NORAH.

And what inducement is there for a girl to have you?

TROTTER.

That's why he wants to catch 'em young, when they've just landed and don't know much.

TAYLOR.

I've got my quarter section—a hundred and sixty acres, with seventy of it cleared—and I've got a shack that I built myself. That's something, ain't it?

NORAH.

You've got a home to offer and enough to eat and drink. A girl can get that anywhere. Why, they're simply begging for service.

TAYLOR.

Some girls like getting married. There's something in the word that appeals to them.

NORAH.

You seem to think a girl would jump at the chance of marrying you.

TAYLOR.

She might do worse.

NORAH.

I think you flatter yourself.

TAYLOR.

I know my job and there ain't too many as can say that. I've got brains.

NORAH.

What makes you think so?

TAYLOR.

Well, I can see you're no fool.

GERTIE.

[*With a chuckle.*] He put one over on you then, Norah.

TAYLOR.

[*Good-humouredly.*] Because you've got no use for me, there's no saying but what others may have.

[GERTIE *takes the basin out in order to pour away the water.* NORAH *goes on drying the crockery.*]

NORAH.

Of course, there's no accounting for tastes.

TAYLOR.

I can try, can't I?

NORAH.

It's very wise of you to go to an agency. A girl's more likely to marry you when she's only seen you once than when she's seen you often.

TAYLOR.

[*With a wink at the others.*] It seems to make you quite mad, the thought of me marrying.

NORAH.

You wouldn't talk about it like that unless you looked down upon women. Oh, I pity the poor wretched creature who becomes your wife.

TAYLOR.

I guess she won't have a bad time when I've broken her in to my ways.

NORAH.

Are you under the impression you can do that?

TAYLOR.

Yep.

NORAH.

You're not expecting that there'll be much love lost between you and the girl you—honour with your choice?

TAYLOR.

What's love got to do with it? It's a business proposition.

NORAH.

What!

TAYLOR.

I give her board and lodging and the charm of my society. And in return she's got to cook and bake and wash and keep the shack clean and tidy. And if she can do that I'll not be particular what she looks like.

MARSH.

So long as she's not cock-eyed.

TAYLOR.

No, I draw the line at that.

NORAH.

[*Ironically.*] I beg your pardon. I didn't know it was a general servant you wanted. You spend a dollar and a half on a marriage licence, and then you don't have to pay any wages. It's a good investment.

TAYLOR.

You've got a sharp tongue in your head for a girl, Norah.

NORAH.

Please don't call me Norah.

MARSH.

Don't be so silly. It's the custom of the country. Why, they all call me Ed.

NORAH.

- 38 -

I don't care what the custom of the country is. I'm not going to be called Norah by the hired man.

TAYLOR.

Don't you bother, Ed. I'll call her Miss Marsh if she likes it better.

NORAH.

I should like to see you married to someone who'd give you what you deserved. I'd like to see your pride humbled. You think yourself very high and mighty, don't you? I'd like to see a woman take you by the heart-strings and wring them till you screamed with pain.

MARSH.

[*With a laugh.*] Norah, how violent you are.

NORAH.

You're overbearing, supercilious, egotistic.

TAYLOR.

I'm not sure as I know what them long words means, but I guess they ain't exactly complimentary.

NORAH.

[*Furiously.*] I guess they ain't.

TAYLOR.

I'm sorry for that. I was thinking of offering you the position before I went to the employment agency.

NORAH.

How dare you speak to me like that!

MARSH.

Don't fly into a temper, Norah.

NORAH.

He's got no right to say impudent things to me.

MARSH.

Don't you see he's only having a joke with you?

NORAH.

He shouldn't joke. He's got no sense of humour.

[NORAH *drops a cup and breaks it, and as this happens* GERTIE *comes in.*]

GERTIE.

Butter fingers.

NORAH.

I'm so sorry.

GERTIE.

You clumsy thing. You're always doing something wrong.

NORAH.

You needn't worry, I'll pay for it.

GERTIE.

Who wants you to pay for it? D'you think I can't afford to pay for a cup? You might say you're sorry—that's all I want you to do.

NORAH.

I said I was sorry.

GERTIE.

No, you didn't.

MARSH.

I heard her, Gertie.

GERTIE.

She said she was sorry as if she was doing me a favour.

NORAH.

You don't expect me to go down on my knees to you? The cup's worth twopence.

GERTIE.

It isn't the value I'm thinking about, it's the carelessness.

NORAH.

It's only the third thing I've broken since I've been here.

GERTIE.

You can't do anything; you're more helpless than a child of six. You're all the same, all of you.

NORAH.

You're not going to abuse the whole British nation because I've broken a cup worth twopence, are you?

GERTIE.

And the airs you put on. Condescending isn't the word. It's enough to try the patience of a saint.

MARSH.

Oh, shut up.

GERTIE.

You've never done a stroke of work in your life, and you come here and think you can teach me everything.

NORAH.

I don't know about that, but I think I can teach you manners.

GERTIE.

How dare you say that! How dare you! You come here and I give you a home, you sleep in my blankets and eat my food, and then you insult me.

[*She bursts into tears.*]

MARSH.

Now then, Gertie, don't cry. Don't be so silly.

GERTIE.

Oh, leave me alone. Of course you take her part. You would. It's nothing to you that I've slaved for you for three years. As soon as she comes along and plays the lady....

[*She hurries out of the room.* MARSH *hesitates for a moment and then follows his wife. There is a momentary pause.*]

TAYLOR.

I reckon I might be cleaning myself. Time's getting on. You're coming, Ben?

TROTTER.

Yes, I'm coming. I suppose you'll take the mare?

TAYLOR.

Yep. That's what Ed said this morning.

[*They go out.* NORAH *is left alone with* REGGIE HORNBY.]

HORNBY.

[*With a little smile.*] Well, are you enjoying the land of promise as much as you said I should?

NORAH.

We've both made our bed and we must lie in it.

HORNBY.

D'you remember that afternoon at Miss Wickham's when I came for a letter to your brother?

NORAH.

I hadn't much intention of coming to Canada then.

HORNBY.

I don't mind telling you that I mean to get back to England the very first opportunity I get. I'm willing to give away my share of the White Man's Burden with a packet of chewing gum.

NORAH.

[*Smiling.*] You prefer the Effete East?

HORNBY.

Rather. Give me the degrading influence of a decadent civilisation every time.

NORAH.

Your father will be pleased to see you, won't he?

HORNBY.

I don't think. Of course, I was a damned fool ever to leave Winnipeg.

NORAH.

I understand you didn't till you were forced to.

HORNBY.

Your brother behaved like a perfect brick. I sent him on your letter and told him I was up against it—d'you know I hadn't got a bob? I was jolly glad to earn half a dollar by digging a pit in a man's garden. Bit thick, you know.

NORAH.

[*Laughing.*] I can see you.

HORNBY.

Your brother sent me my fare to come here and told me I could do the chores. I didn't know what they were. I found out it was doing all the jobs that it wasn't anybody else's job to do. And they call it God's own country.

[*Meanwhile* NORAH *has put a couple of irons on the stove and now she gets the board. It is rather heavy for her.*]

NORAH.

I think you're falling into the ways very well.

HORNBY.

What makes you think that?

NORAH.

[*With a smile.*] You can sit by and smoke your pipe, and watch me carry the ironing board about.

HORNBY.

[*Without moving.*] D'you want me to help you?

NORAH.

No.... It would remind me of home.

HORNBY.

I suppose I shall have to stick it out at least a year, unless I can humbug the mater into sending me enough money to get home with.

NORAH.

She won't send you a penny if she's wise.

HORNBY.

Wouldn't you chuck it if you could?

NORAH.

[*With a flash of spirit.*] And acknowledge myself beaten? [*There is a short pause.*] You don't know what I went through before I came here. I tried to get another position as lady's companion. I answered advertisements. I hung about the agent's offices.... Two people offered to take me without a salary. One woman suggested ten shillings a week and my lunch. She expected me to find myself a room, clothes, breakfast and supper on ten shillings a week. That settled me. I wrote to Eddie and said I was coming. When I'd paid my fare I had eight pounds in the world. That's the result of ten years' work as lady's companion. When he came to meet me at the station at Dyer....

HORNBY.

Don't call it a station, call it a depôt.

NORAH.

My whole fortune consisted of seven dollars and thirty-five cents.

[MARSH *comes in and gives* HORNBY *a glance.*]

MARSH.

What about that wood you were splitting, Reg? You'd better be getting on with it.

HORNBY.

Oh, lord, is there no rest for the wicked?

[*He gets up slowly and saunters lazily to the door.*]

MARSH.

Don't hurry yourself, will you?

HORNBY.

Brilliant sarcasm is just flying about the house to-day.

[*He goes out.*]

MARSH.

That's about the toughest nut I've ever been set to crack. Why on earth did you give him a letter to me?

NORAH.

He asked me. I couldn't very well say no.

[*Throughout the scene* NORAH *goes on ironing things which she takes from a pile of washing in the basket.*]

MARSH.

I can't make out what people are up to in the Old Country. They think that if a man is too big a rotter to do anything at all in England they've only got to send him out here and he'll make a fortune.

NORAH.

- 44 -

He may improve.

MARSH.

[*With a look at* NORAH.] You've thoroughly upset Gertie.

NORAH.

She's very easily upset, isn't she?

MARSH.

It's only since you came that things haven't gone right. We never used to have scenes.

NORAH.

Do you blame me? I came prepared to like her and help her. She met all my advances with suspicion.

MARSH.

She thinks you look down upon her. You ought to remember that she never had your opportunities. She's earned her own living from the time she was thirteen. You can't expect in her the refinements of a woman who's led the protected life that you have.

NORAH.

I haven't said a word that could be turned into the least suggestion of disapproval of anything she did.

MARSH.

My dear, your whole manner has expressed disapproval. You won't do things in the way we do them. After all, the way you lived in Tunbridge Wells isn't the only way people can live. Our ways suit us, and when you live amongst us you must adopt them.

NORAH.

She never gave me a chance to learn them. She treated me with suspicion and enmity from the very first day I came here. When she sneered at me because I talked of a station instead of a depôt, of course I went on talking of a station. Because I prefer to drink water with my meals instead of strong tea she said I was putting on side.

MARSH.

Why can't you humour her? You see, you've got to take the blame for all the English people who came here in the past and were lazy, worthless, and supercilious. They called us Colonials and turned up their noses at us.

What d'you expect us to do? Say, "Thank you very much, sir; we know we're not worthy to black your boots; and don't bother to work—it'll be a pleasure for us to give you money"? It's no good blinking the fact, there was a great prejudice against the English, but it's giving way now, and every sensible man and woman who comes out can do something to destroy it.

NORAH.

[*With a shrug of the shoulders.*] If you're tired of having me here I can go back to Winnipeg. I shan't have any difficulty in finding something to do.

MARSH.

Good lord, I don't want you to go. I like having you here, and it's company for Gertie. And you know, jobs aren't so easy to find as you think, especially now the winter's coming on. Everyone wants a job in the city.

NORAH.

What d'you want me to do?

MARSH.

Well, you've got to live with Gertie. Why can't you make the best of things and meet her half way? You might make allowances for her even if you think her unreasonable.

NORAH.

I'll have a try.

MARSH.

I think you ought to apologise for what you said to her just now.

NORAH.

I? I've got nothing to apologise for. She drove me to distraction.

[*There is a moment's pause.* MARSH, *now that he has come to the object of all he has been saying, is a little embarrassed.*]

MARSH.

She says she won't speak to you again until you beg her pardon.

NORAH.

Does she look upon that as a great hardship?

MARSH.

My dear, we're twelve miles from the nearest store. We're thrown upon one another through the whole of the winter. Last year there was a

- 46 -

bad blizzard, and for six weeks we didn't see a soul outside the farm. Unless we learn to put up with one another's whims life becomes a perfect hell.

NORAH.

You can go on talking all night, Eddie—I'll never apologise. Time after time when she sneered at me till my blood boiled. I've kept my temper. She deserved ten times more than I said. D'you think I'm going to knuckle under to a woman like that?

MARSH.

Remember she's my wife, Norah.

NORAH.

Why didn't you marry a lady?

MARSH.

What the dickens d'you think is the use of being a lady out here?

NORAH.

You've degenerated since you left England.

MARSH.

Now, look here, my dear, I'll just tell you what Gertie did for me. She was a waitress in Winnipeg at the Minnedosa Hotel, and she was making money. She knew what the life was on a farm, much harder than anything she'd been used to in the city, but she accepted all the hardship of it, and the monotony—because she loved me.

NORAH.

She thought it a good match. You were a gentleman.

MARSH.

Fiddledidee. She had the chance of much better men than me.... And when I lost my harvest two years running, d'you know what she did? She went back to the hotel in Winnipeg for the winter so as to carry things on till the next harvest. And at the end of the winter she gave me every cent she'd earned to pay the interest of my mortgage and the instalments on the machinery.

[*There is a pause.*]

NORAH.

Very well, I'll apologise. But leave me alone with her. I—I don't think I could do it before anyone else.

MARSH.

All right. I'll go and tell her.

[*He goes out.* NORAH *is left alone with her thoughts. In a moment* GERTIE *comes back, followed by* MARSH.]

NORAH.

[*Trying to take things lightly.*] I've been getting on with the ironing.

GERTIE.

Have you?

NORAH.

[*With a smile.*] That is one of the few things I can do all right.

GERTIE.

Any child can iron.

MARSH.

Well, I'll be going down to the shed.

GERTIE.

[*Turning to him quickly.*] What for?

MARSH.

I want to see about mending that door. It hasn't been closing properly.

GERTIE.

I thought Norah had something to say to me.

MARSH.

That's what I'm going to leave you alone for.

GERTIE.

I like that. She insults me before everybody and then when she's going to apologise it's got to be private. No, thank you.

NORAH.

What d'you mean, Gertie?

GERTIE.

You sent Ed in to tell me you was going to apologise for what you'd said, didn't you?

NORAH.

For peace and quietness.

GERTIE.

Well, what you said was before the men, and it's before the men you must say you're sorry.

NORAH.

How can you ask me to do such a thing!

MARSH.

Don't be rough on her, Gertie. No one likes apologising.

GERTIE.

People who don't like apologising should keep a better lookout on their tongue.

MARSH.

It can't do you any good to have her eat humble pie before the men.

GERTIE.

Perhaps not, but it'll do her good.

NORAH.

Gertie, don't be cruel. I'm sorry if I lost my temper just now and said anything that hurt you. Please don't make me humiliate myself before the others.

GERTIE.

I've made up my mind, so it's no good talking.

NORAH.

Don't you see it's bad enough to beg your pardon before Eddie?

GERTIE.

[*Irritably.*] Why don't you call him Ed like the rest of us? Eddie sounds so soppy.

NORAH.

I've called him Eddie all my life.... It's what his mother called him.

GERTIE.

You do everything you can to make yourself different from all of us.

NORAH.

No, I don't, I promise you I don't. Why won't you give me any credit for trying to do my best to please you?

GERTIE.

That's neither here nor there. Go and fetch the men, Ed, and then I'll hear what she's got to say.

NORAH.

No, I won't, I won't, I won't. You drive me too far.

GERTIE.

You won't beg my pardon?

NORAH.

[*Beside herself.*] I said I could teach you manners. I made a mistake, I couldn't teach you manners. One can't make a silk purse out of a sow's ear.

MARSH.

[*Sharply.*] Shut up, Norah.

GERTIE.

Now you must make her, Ed.

MARSH.

I'm sick to death of the pair of you.

GERTIE.

I'm your wife, and I'm going to be mistress of this house.

MARSH.

It's horrible to make her eat humble pie before three strange men. You've got no right to ask her to do a thing like that.

GERTIE.

[*Furiously.*] Are you taking her part? What's come over you since she come here? You're not the same to me as you used to be. Why did she come here and get between us?

MARSH.

I haven't done anything.

GERTIE.

Haven't I been a good wife to you? Have you ever had any complaint to make about me?

MARSH.

You know I haven't.

GERTIE.

As soon as your sister comes along you let me be insulted. You don't say a word to defend me.

MARSH.

[*With a grim smile.*] Darling, you've said a good many to defend yourself.

GERTIE.

I'm sick and tired of being put upon. You must choose between us.

MARSH.

What on earth d'you mean?

GERTIE.

If you don't make her apologise right now before the hired men I'm quit of you.

MARSH.

I can't make her apologise if she won't.

GERTIE.

Then let her quit.

NORAH.

Oh, I wish I could. I wish to God I could.

MARSH.

You know she can't do that. There's nowhere she can go. I've offered her a home. You were quite willing when I suggested having her here.

GERTIE.

I was willing because I thought she'd make herself useful. We can't afford to feed folks as don't earn their keep. We have to work for our money, we do.

NORAH.

I didn't know you grudged me the little I eat. I wonder if I should if I were in your place.

MARSH.

Look here, it's no good talking. I'm not going to turn her out. As long as she wants a home the farm's open to her. And she's welcome to everything I've got.

GERTIE.

Then you choose her?

MARSH.

[*Irritably.*] I don't know what you're talking about.

GERTIE.

I said you'd got to choose between us. Very well. Let her stay. I earned my living before, and I can earn it again. I'm going.

MARSH.

Don't talk such nonsense.

GERTIE.

You think I don't mean it? D'you think I'm going to stay here and be put upon? Why should I?

MARSH.

Don't you—love me any more?

GERTIE.

Haven't I shown that I love you? Have you forgotten, Ed?

MARSH.

We've gone through so much together, darling.

GERTIE.

[*Hesitatingly.*] Yes, we have that.

MARSH.

Won't you forgive her?

GERTIE.

No, I can't. You're a man, you don't understand. If she won't apologise, either she must go or I shall.

MARSH.

I can't lose you, Gertie. What should I do without you?

GERTIE.

I guess you know me well enough by now. When I say a thing I do it.

NORAH.

Eddie.

MARSH.

[*Ill at ease.*] After all, she's my wife. If it weren't for her I should be hiring out now at forty dollars a month.

[NORAH *hesitates for a moment, then she makes up her mind.*]

NORAH.

[*Hoarsely.*] Very well, I'll do what you want.

MARSH.

You do insist on it, Gertie?

GERTIE.

Of course I do.

MARSH.

I'll go and call the men.

NORAH.

Frank Taylor needn't come, need he?

GERTIE.

Why not?

NORAH.

He's going away to-day. It can't much matter about him, surely.

GERTIE.

Why are you so particular about it, then?

NORAH.

The others are English. He'll like to see me humiliated. He looks upon women as dirt. He's.... Oh, I don't know, but not before him.

GERTIE.

It'll do you a world of good to be taken down a peg or two, my lady.

NORAH.

Oh, how heartless—how cruel.

GERTIE.

Go on, Ed—I want to get on with my work.

[MARSH *hesitates a moment, then shrugs his shoulders and goes out.*]

NORAH.

[*Passionately.*] Why do you humiliate me like this?

GERTIE.

You came here and thought you knew everything, I guess. You didn't know who you'd got to deal with.

NORAH.

I was a stranger and homeless. If you'd had any kindness you wouldn't have treated me so. I wanted to be fond of you.

GERTIE.

You despised me before you ever saw me.

[NORAH *covers her eyes for a moment with both hands, and then forces herself to make another appeal.*]

NORAH.

Oh, Gertie, can't we be friends? Can't we let bygones be bygones and start afresh? We're both fond of Eddie. He's your husband and you love him, and he's the only relation I have in the world. Won't you let me be a real sister to you?

GERTIE.

It's rather late to say all that now.

NORAH.

But it's not too late, is it? I don't know what I do that irritates you. I can see how competent you are, and I admire you so much. I know how splendid you've been with Eddie, and how you've stuck to him through thick and thin. You've done everything for him.

GERTIE.

[*Breaking in violently.*] Oh, don't go on patronising me. I shall go crazy.

NORAH.

[*Astounded.*] Patronising you?

GERTIE.

You talk to me as if I was a naughty child. You might be a school teacher.

NORAH.

It seems perfectly hopeless.

GERTIE.

Even when you're begging my pardon you put on airs. You ask me to forgive you as if you was doing me a favour.

NORAH.

[*With a chuckle.*] I must have a very unfortunate manner.

GERTIE.

[*Furiously.*] Don't laugh at me.

NORAH.

Don't make yourself ridiculous, then.

GERTIE.

D'you think I shall ever forget what you wrote to Ed before I married him?

NORAH.

[*Looking at her quickly.*] I don't know what you mean.

GERTIE.

Don't you? You told him it would be a disgrace if he married me. He was a gentleman and I.... Oh, you spread yourself out.

NORAH.

He oughtn't to have shown you the letter.

GERTIE.

He was dotty about me.

NORAH.

I had a perfect right to try and prevent the marriage before it took place. But after it happened I only wanted to make the best of it. If you had a grudge against me why did you let me come here?

GERTIE.

Ed wanted it, and it was lonely enough sometimes with the men away all day and no one to talk to. I thought you'd be company for me.... I can't bear it when Ed talks to you about the Old Country and people I don't know nothing about.

NORAH.

[*Surprised.*] Are you jealous?

GERTIE.

It's my house and I'm mistress here. I won't be put upon. What did you want to come here for, upsetting everybody? Till you come I never had a word with Ed. Oh, I hate you, I hate you.

NORAH.

Gertie.

GERTIE.

You've given me a chance and I'm going to take it. I'm going to take you down a peg or two.

NORAH.

You're doing all you can to drive me away from here.

GERTIE.

You don't think it's much catch to have you. You talk of getting a job—you couldn't get one. I know something about that, my girl. You! You can do nothing.... Here they are. Now take your medicine.

[ED MARSH *comes in, followed by* TROTTER *and* FRANK TAYLOR. FRANK *has taken off his overalls.*]

GERTIE.

Where's Reg?

MARSH.

He's just coming.

GERTIE.

Do they know what they're here for?

- 56 -

MARSH.

No, I didn't tell them.

[HORNBY *comes in.*]

GERTIE.

Norah insulted me a while ago before all of you, and I guess she wants to apologise.

TAYLOR.

If you told me it was that, Ed, you wanted me to come here for, I reckon I'd have told you to go to hell.

NORAH.

Why?

TAYLOR.

I've got other things to do beside bothering my head about women's quarrels.

NORAH.

Oh, I beg your pardon, I thought it was some kindly feeling in you.

GERTIE.

Go on, Norah, we're waiting.

[NORAH *hesitates a moment and then takes her courage in both hands.*]

NORAH.

I'm sorry I was rude to you, Gertie. I apologise for what I said.

TAYLOR.

[*With a quiet smile.*] You didn't find that very easy to say, I reckon.

MARSH.

There's nothing more to be said, is there?

GERTIE.

I'm quite satisfied.

MARSH.

We'd better get back to work, then.

[*The men turn to go.*]

- 57 -

GERTIE.

Let this be a lesson to you, my girl.

[NORAH *starts at the words. It is the last straw.*]

NORAH.

Frank, will you wait a minute?

TAYLOR.

[*A little surprised.*] Sure. What can I do for you?

NORAH.

I've understood that I'm not wanted here. I'm in the way. You said just now you wanted a woman to cook and bake for you, wash and mend your clothes, and keep your shack clean and tidy. Will I do?

TAYLOR.

[*Rather amused.*] Sure.

MARSH.

[*Horrified.*] Norah.

NORAH.

[*With a twinkle in her eye.*] I'm afraid you'll have to marry me.

TAYLOR.

I guess it would be more respectable.

MARSH.

Norah, you can't mean it. You're in a temper. See here, Frank, you mustn't pay any attention to her.

GERTIE.

Shameless, that's what I call it.

NORAH.

Why? He wants a woman to look after him. He practically proposed to me half an hour ago. Didn't you?

TAYLOR.

Practically.

HORNBY.

I'm bound to say I've never heard a proposal refused so emphatically.

MARSH.

You've been like cat and dog with Frank ever since you came. My dear, you don't know what you're in for.

NORAH.

If he's willing to risk it, I am.

TAYLOR.

[*Looking at her gravely.*] It ain't an easy life you're coming to. This farm's a palace compared with my shack.

NORAH.

I'm not wanted here, and you say you want me. If you'll take me, I'll come.

TAYLOR.

I'll take you all right. When will you be ready? Will an hour do for you?

NORAH.

[*Suddenly panic-stricken.*] An hour?

TAYLOR.

Why, yes, then we can catch the three-thirty into Winnipeg. You can go to the Y.W.C.A. for the night and we'll be buckled up in the morning.

NORAH.

You're in a great hurry.

TAYLOR.

I suppose you meant it? You weren't just pulling a bluff?

[NORAH *hesitates for a moment and they look at one another.*]

NORAH.

I shall be ready in an hour.

END OF THE SECOND ACT

ACT III

SCENE: FRANK TAYLOR'S *shack at Prentice, Manitoba. It is a low log cabin, consisting of two rooms. The scene is the living-room. There is a door at the back towards the left-hand side, and on the right is another door that leads into the bedroom. A very small low window at the back. There is a stove on the left, with a long chimney. On the walls, untidily tacked up, are pictures cut out of the illustrated papers. Hanging on a nail is a Cariboo coat. On a shelf beside the stove are the few pots and pans that FRANK TAYLOR possesses. They are battered and much used. There is a broom in the corner. The furniture consists of a rocking-chair, worn with use and shabby, a table roughly made by TAYLOR himself from packing-cases, one kitchen chair and two or three packing-cases used as stools. On another shelf are maple-syrup tins, in which groceries are kept. In one corner there is an old suit-case, locally known as a grip, and a heap of old clothes; in another corner is a pile of tattered magazines and numbers of the Winnipeg Free Press. The shack has an untidy, comfortless, bedraggled air.*

When the curtain rises the scene is dark and empty. There is a faint glimmer of light through the window. The night is bright and starry. There is a slight noise of a rig being driven up outside, and then voices are heard.

SHARP.

Woa there! Woa!

TAYLOR.

A tidy pull, that last bit. Trail's very bad.

SHARP.

Stop still, you brute.

TAYLOR.

I guess she wants to get home.

[*Now comes the sound of a key being put into the lock. It is turned noisily and the door is opened wide. A rig stands outside and SHARP is seen still seated holding the reins. NORAH has just got down. Tied on the back of the rig are NORAH'S trunk and TAYLOR'S grip. There is a glimpse of the prairie and the bright Canadian night. TAYLOR comes in. He is wearing a waterproof coat lined with sheepskin, a dark, roughly cut suit of some coarse blue material, and a broad-brimmed, flat-crowned hat.*]

TAYLOR.

Wait a minute, and I'll light the lamp. [*He strikes a match and looks round.*] Where in hell has it got to? The shack's about two foot by three, and I'm blamed if I can ever find a darned thing.

SHARP.

I'll give you a hand with that trunk.

[*As he speaks he begins to get down.* TAYLOR *finds the lamp and lights it.*]

TAYLOR.

I'll come and help you if you'll wait a bit. Come in, Norah.

SHARP.

Woa there!

[NORAH *comes in. She has on a hat and coat. She carries a string bag in which there is a number of parcels.*]

NORAH.

I'm quite stiff after that long drive.

TAYLOR.

Are you cold?

NORAH.

No, not a bit. I was well wrapped up.

TAYLOR.

I guess it's freezing. But it's your first winter and you won't feel the cold like we do.

NORAH.

[*Putting down her bag.*] I'll bring some of the things in.

TAYLOR.

Don't touch the trunk, it's too heavy for you.

NORAH.

I'm as strong as a horse.

TAYLOR.

Don't touch it.

NORAH.

[*With a smile.*] I won't.

- 61 -

[*He goes out and takes more parcels out of the rig and comes in with them.*]

TAYLOR.

We can all do with a cup of tea. Just have a look at the stove. It won't take two shakes to light a fire.

NORAH.

It seems hardly worth while. It's so late.

TAYLOR.

[*Cheerily.*] Light the fire, my girl, and don't talk about it.

[*He goes out and is seen helping* SHARP *to unfasten the trunk.* NORAH, *getting down on her knees, rakes out the ashes from the stove.* TAYLOR *and* SHARP *bring the box in between them.* SHARP *is a rough-looking man of forty. He has been a non-commissioned officer in an English regiment, and has still something of a soldier's look.*]

SHARP.

This trunk of yours isn't what you might call light, Mrs. Taylor.

NORAH.

It contains all I own in the world.

TAYLOR.

I guess it don't do that. Since this morning you own a half share in a hundred and sixty acres of as good land as there is in Manitoba and a mighty fine shack.

NORAH.

To say nothing of a husband.

SHARP.

Where d'you want this put?

TAYLOR.

It 'ud better go in the next room right away, or we shall be falling over it.

[*They carry the trunk into the bedroom.* NORAH *gets up from her knees, goes over to a pile of logs by the stove, and takes two or three and some of the newspapers. The men come in again.*]

TAYLOR.

Here, you won't be able to light a fire with logs like that. Where's that darned axe? [*He glances round and sees it by the logs. He takes a couple and splits them.*] I guess you'll have plenty to do getting the shack tidy. [SHARP *brings in* TAYLOR'S *grip and his gun.*] Now, that's real good of you, Sid.

SHARP.

Get any shooting down at Dyer, Frank?

TAYLOR.

There was a rare lot of prairie chickens around, but I didn't get out more than a couple of days.

SHARP.

Well, I'll be getting back home now.

TAYLOR.

Oh, stay and have a cup of tea, won't you?

SHARP.

I don't think I will. It's getting late and the mare'll get cold.

TAYLOR.

Put her in the shed.

SHARP.

No, I think I'll be toddling. My missus says I was to give you her compliments, Mrs. Taylor, and she'll be round to-morrow to see if there's anything you want.

NORAH.

That's very kind of her. Thank you very much.

TAYLOR.

Sid lives where you saw that light just about a mile from here, Norah. Mrs. Sharp'll be able to help you a lot at first.

SHARP.

Oh, well, we've been here for thirteen years, and we know the way of the country by now.

TAYLOR.

Norah's about as green as a new dollar bill, I guess.

SHARP.

There's a lot you can't be expected to know at first. I'll say good-night, then, and good luck.

TAYLOR.

Well, good-night then, Sid, if you won't stay, and it was real good of you to come and fetch us in the rig.

SHARP.

Oh, that's all right. Good-night to you, Mrs. Taylor.

NORAH.

Good-night.

[SHARP *goes out, gets on the rig, and drives away.*]

TAYLOR.

I guess it must seem funny to you to hear him call you Mrs. Taylor, eh?

[NORAH *gives him a quick look, and represses a little shudder.*]

NORAH.

Yes.

TAYLOR.

How are you getting on with that fire?

NORAH.

All right.

TAYLOR.

I guess I'll get some water.

[He *takes a pail and goes out. He is heard pumping.* NORAH *gets up, lifts the lamp so as to see better, and looks round. She is pale, and has a frightened look. She does not hear* FRANK *come in, and starts violently when he speaks to her.*]

TAYLOR.

Having a look at the shack?

NORAH.

[*Putting the lamp down.*] How you startled me.

TAYLOR.

What d'you think of it?

- 64 -

NORAH.

I don't know.

TAYLOR.

I built it with my own hands. Every one of them logs was a tree I cut down myself. You wait till the morning and I'll show you how they're joined together at the corners. There's some neat work there, my girl, I guess.

NORAH.

Here's the kettle.

[*He pours water into it from the pail, and she puts the kettle on the stove.*]

TAYLOR.

You'll find some tea in one of them tins on the shelf. Leastways there was some there when I come away. I guess you're hungry.

NORAH.

I don't think I am, very. I ate a very good supper in the train.

TAYLOR.

I'm glad you call that a good supper. I guess I could wrap up the amount you ate in a postal stamp.

NORAH.

[*Smiling.*] I haven't a very large appetite.

TAYLOR.

I have. Where's the loaf we got in Winnipeg this afternoon?

NORAH.

I'll get it.

TAYLOR.

And the butter. You'll bake to-morrow, I reckon.

[NORAH *gets a loaf and a piece of butter out of the string bag she brought in with her. She puts them on the table.*]

NORAH.

Shall I cut you some?

TAYLOR.

Yep.

NORAH.

Please.

TAYLOR.

Please what?

NORAH.

[*With a smile.*] Yes, please.

TAYLOR.

Oh!

[*He gives her a look, and she, a quiet smile on her face, cuts two or three pieces of bread and butter. Then she gets tea out of the tin and puts it in a teapot.*]

TAYLOR.

I guess you'd better take your hat and coat off.

[NORAH *does so without answering.*]

TAYLOR.

You ain't terribly talkative for a woman, my girl.

NORAH.

I haven't got anything to say at the moment.

TAYLOR.

Well, I guess it's better to have a wife as talks too little than a wife as talks too much.

NORAH.

[*With her tongue in her cheek.*] I suppose absolute perfection is rare—in women, poor wretches.

TAYLOR.

What's that?

NORAH.

I was only amusing myself with a reflection.

[TAYLOR *takes off his coat and appears in a grey sweater. He sits down in the rocking chair.*]

TAYLOR.

- 66 -

I guess there's no place like home. You get a bit fed up with hiring out. Ed was O.K., I reckon, but it ain't like being your own boss.

NORAH.

[*Pointing.*] What's through there?

TAYLOR.

Oh, that's the bedroom. Like to have a look?

NORAH.

No.

TAYLOR.

When I built the shack I fixed it up so as it would do when I got married. Sid Sharp asked me what in hell I wanted to divide it up in half for, but I guess women like little luxuries like that.

NORAH.

Like what?

TAYLOR.

Like having a room to sleep in and a room to live in.

NORAH.

Here's the bread and butter. Will you have some syrup?

TAYLOR.

Sure.

[*He gets up and sits down at the table.*]

NORAH.

That water ought to be boiling by now. What about milk?

TAYLOR.

That's one of the things you'll have to do without till I can afford to buy a cow.

NORAH.

I can't drink tea without milk.

TAYLOR.

You try. Say, can you milk a cow?

NORAH.

I? No.

TAYLOR.

Then it's just as well I ain't got one.

NORAH.

You're a philosopher.

[*She lifts the cover off the kettle and looks at it, then pours some water into the teapot, and sets it down on the table.*]

NORAH.

Is there a candle? I'll just get one or two things out of my box.

TAYLOR.

Ain't you going to sit down and have a cup of tea?

NORAH.

I don't want any, thanks.

TAYLOR.

Sit down, my girl.

NORAH.

Why?

TAYLOR.

[*Smiling.*] Because I tell you to.

NORAH.

[*Quite pleasantly.*] I don't think you'd better tell me to do things.

TAYLOR.

Then I ask you. You ain't going to refuse the first favour I've asked you?

NORAH.

[*With a pretty smile.*] Of course not. [*She sits down.*] There.

TAYLOR.

Now pour out my tea for me, will you? [*He watches her do it.*] It is rum seeing my wife sitting down at my table and pouring out tea for me.

NORAH.

Is it pleasant?

TAYLOR.

Sure. Now have some yourself, my girl. You'll soon get used to drinking it without milk. And I guess you'll be able to get some to-morrow from Mrs. Sharp.

[NORAH *pours herself out some tea.*]

TAYLOR.

I had a sort of a feeling I wanted you and me to have the first meal together in your new home. Just take a bit of the bread and butter.

[*He passes over to her a slice and, smiling, she cuts a little piece off and eats it.*]

TAYLOR.

We ain't lost much time, I guess. Why, it's only yesterday you told me not to call you Norah.

NORAH.

That was very silly of me. I was in a temper.

TAYLOR.

And now we're man and wife.

NORAH.

Married in haste with a vengeance.

TAYLOR.

Ain't you a bit scared?

NORAH.

I? What of? You?

TAYLOR.

With Ed on t'other side of Winnipeg, he might just as well be in the Old Country for all the good he can be to you. You might be a bit scared to find yourself alone with a man you don't know.

NORAH.

I'm not nervous.

TAYLOR.

Good for you.

NORAH.

You did give me a fright, though. When I asked you if you'd take me, I suppose it was only about fifteen seconds before you answered, but it seemed like ten minutes. I thought you might refuse.

TAYLOR.

I was thinking.

NORAH.

[*Smiling.*] Counting up my good points and setting them against the bad ones?

TAYLOR.

No, I was thinking you wouldn't have asked me like that if you hadn't—despised me.

[NORAH, *a little taken aback, gives him a quick look, but she tries to pass it off lightly.*]

NORAH.

I don't know what makes you think that.

TAYLOR.

Well, I don't know how you could have put it more plainly that my name was mud.

NORAH.

Why didn't you refuse, then?

TAYLOR.

I guess I'm not a nervous fellow, either.

NORAH.

[*With a twinkle in her eye.*] And women are scarce in Manitoba.

TAYLOR.

I always fancied an Englishwoman. They make the best wives when they've been licked into shape.

NORAH.

[*Frankly amused.*] Are you proposing to attempt that operation on me?

TAYLOR.

You're clever. I guess a hint or two is about all you'll want.

NORAH.

It embarrasses me when you pay me compliments.

TAYLOR.

I'll take you round and show you the land to-morrow. I ain't done all the clearing yet, so there'll be plenty of work for the winter. I want to have a hundred acres to sow next year. And then if I get a good crop I've a mind to take another quarter. You can't make it pay really without you've got half a section. And it's a tough proposition when you ain't got capital.

NORAH.

I didn't think I was marrying a millionaire.

TAYLOR.

Never mind, my girl, you shan't live in a shack long, I promise you. It's the greatest country in the world. We only want three good crops and you shall have a brick house same as you lived in at home.

NORAH.

I wonder what they're doing in England now.

TAYLOR.

Well, I guess they're asleep.

NORAH.

When I think of England I always think of it at tea-time. [*She looks at the tea-things they have just used.*] Miss Wickham had a beautiful old silver teapot—George II.—and she was awfully proud of it. And she was very proud of her tea-set—it was old Worcester—and she wouldn't let anyone wash the things but.... And two or three times a week an old Indian judge came in to tea, and he used to talk to me about the East—oh, why did you make me think of it all?

TAYLOR.

The past is dead and gone, my girl. We've got the future.

NORAH.

[*Paying no attention to his words.*] One never knows when one's well off, does one? It's madness to think of what's gone for ever.

TAYLOR.

I wish we'd got a drop of liquor here so as we could drink one another's health. But as we ain't you'd better give me a kiss instead.

NORAH.

[*Lightly.*] I'm not very fond of kissing.

TAYLOR.

[*With a smile.*] It ain't generally an acquired taste, but I guess you're peculiar.

NORAH.

It looks like it.

TAYLOR.

Come, my girl, you didn't even kiss me after we was married.

NORAH.

[*In a perfectly friendly way.*] Isn't a hint enough for you? Why do you force me to say everything in so many words?

TAYLOR.

It seems to me it wants a few words to make it plain when a woman refuses to give her husband a kiss.

NORAH.

Do sit down, there's a good fellow, and I'll tell you one or two things.

TAYLOR.

That's terribly kind of you. [*He sinks back into the rocking-chair.*] Have you any choice of seats?

NORAH.

You've taken the only one that's tolerably comfortable. I think there's nothing to choose between the others.

TAYLOR.

Nothing.

NORAH.

I think we'd better fix things up before we go any further.

TAYLOR.

Sure.

NORAH.

You gave me to understand very plainly that you wanted a wife in order to get a general servant without having to pay her wages. Wages are high in Canada.

TAYLOR.

That was the way you put it.

NORAH.

Baching isn't very comfortable.

TAYLOR.

Not very.

NORAH.

You wanted someone to cook and bake for you, wash, sweep, and mend. I offered to come and do all that. It never struck me for an instant that there was any possibility of your expecting anything else of me.

TAYLOR.

Then you're a damned fool, my girl.

NORAH.

[*Firing up.*] D'you mind not saying things like that to me?

TAYLOR.

[*Good-humouredly.*] I guess I shall have to say a good many things like that before we've done.

NORAH.

I asked you to marry me only because I couldn't stay in the shack without.

TAYLOR.

I guess you asked me to marry you because you was in a hell of a temper. You wanted to get away from Ed's farm right then, and you didn't care what you did so long as you quit. But you was darned sorry for what you'd done by the time you'd packed your box.

NORAH.

[*Frigidly.*] What makes you think that?

TAYLOR.

Why, when you come back in the kitchen you was as white as a sheet. You wanted to say you'd changed your mind, but your darned pride wouldn't let you.

NORAH.

I wouldn't have stayed on in that house for anything in the world.

TAYLOR.

And this morning, when I called for you at the Y.W.C.A., you wanted to say you wouldn't marry me. You tried to speak the words, but they wouldn't come. When you shook hands with me your hand was like ice.

NORAH.

I was nervous for a moment. After all, one isn't married every day of one's life, is one?

TAYLOR.

If I hadn't shown you the licence and the ring, I guess you wouldn't have done it. You hadn't the nerve to back out of it then.

NORAH.

I hadn't slept a wink all night. I kept on turning it over in my mind. I was frightened at what I'd done. But I didn't know a soul in Winnipeg. I hadn't anywhere to go. I had four dollars in my pocket. I had to go through with it.

TAYLOR.

You took pretty good stock of me in the train on the way here, I guess.

NORAH.

[*Recovering herself.*] What makes you think so?

TAYLOR.

Well, I felt you was looking at me a good deal. It wasn't hard to see that you was turning me over in your mind. What conclusion did you come to?

NORAH.

You see, I lived all those years with an old lady. I know very little about men.

TAYLOR.

I guessed that.

NORAH.

I came to the conclusion that you were a decent fellow. I thought you would be kind to me.

TAYLOR.

Bouquets are just flying around. Have you got anything more to say to me?

NORAH.

No.

TAYLOR.

Then just get me my pouch, will you? I guess it's in the pocket of my coat.

[*She hesitates a moment, looks at him, then gets it.*]

NORAH.

Here you are.

TAYLOR.

[*With his tongue in his cheek.*] I thought you was going to tell me I could darned well get it myself.

NORAH.

I don't very much like being ordered about.

TAYLOR.

You never paid much attention to me till to-day, I reckon.

NORAH.

I was always polite to you.

TAYLOR.

Very. But I was the hired man, and you never let me forget it. You thought yourself a darned sight better than me because you could play the piano and speak French. But we ain't got a piano, and there ain't anyone as speaks French nearer than Winnipeg.

NORAH.

What are you driving at?

TAYLOR.

Parlour tricks ain't much good on the prairie. They're like dollar bills up in Hudson Bay. Tobacco's the only thing you can trade with an Esquimaux. You can't cook very well, you don't know how to milk a cow— why, you can't even harness a horse.

NORAH.

Are you regretting your bargain already?

TAYLOR.

No, I guess I can teach you. But if I was you I wouldn't put on any frills. We shall get along O.K., I guess, when we've shaken down.

NORAH.

You'll find I'm perfectly capable of taking care of myself.

TAYLOR.

[*Ignoring the remark.*] When two people live together in a shack there's got to be a deal of give and take on both sides. As long as you do what I tell you you'll be all right.

NORAH.

[*With a smile.*] It's unfortunate that when anyone tells me to do a thing I have an irresistible desire not to do it.

TAYLOR.

I guess I tumbled to that. You must get over it.

NORAH.

You've talked to me once or twice in a way I don't like. I think we shall get on better if you *ask* me to do things.

TAYLOR.

Don't forget that I can *make* you do them.

NORAH.

[*Amused.*] How?

TAYLOR.

Well, I'm stronger than you are.

NORAH.

A man can hardly use force in his dealings with a woman.

TAYLOR.

Oh?

NORAH.

You seem surprised.

TAYLOR.

What's going to prevent him?

NORAH.

[*With a little laugh.*] Don't be so silly.

[*He gives her a look and then smiles quietly to himself.*]

TAYLOR.

Well, I'm going to unpack my grip. [*Pointing to the tea-things.*] Wash up them things.

NORAH.

[*With a slight shrug of the shoulders.*] I'll wash them up in the morning.

TAYLOR.

Wash 'em up now, my girl. You'll find the only way to keep things clean is to wash 'em the moment you've done with them.

[NORAH *looks at him with a slight smile on her face, but does not move.*]

TAYLOR.

Did you hear what I said?

NORAH.

I did.

TAYLOR.

Why don't you do as I tell you?

NORAH.

[*Smiling.*] Because I don't choose.

TAYLOR.

You ain't taken long to try it out.

NORAH.

They say there's no time like the present.

TAYLOR.

Are you going to wash up them things?

NORAH.

No.

[*He looks at her for a moment, then gets up, pours water into a pail and puts a ragged dishcloth on the table.*]

TAYLOR.

Are you going to wash up them things?

NORAH.

No.

TAYLOR.

D'you want me to make you?

NORAH.

How can you do that?

TAYLOR.

I'll show you.

NORAH.

I'll just get out these rugs, shall I? I expect it gets very cold towards morning.

[*She gets up and goes over to a holdall and begins unstrapping it.*]

TAYLOR.

Norah.

NORAH.

Yes.

TAYLOR.

Come here.

NORAH.

Why?

TAYLOR.

Because I tell you.

[*She looks at him, but does not move. He goes over to her and is about to seize her wrist.*]

NORAH.

You daren't touch me.

TAYLOR.

Who told you that?

NORAH.

Have you forgotten that I'm a woman?

TAYLOR.

No, I haven't. That's why I'm going to make you do as I tell you. If you was a man I mightn't be able to. Come now.

[*He makes a movement to take her by the arm, but she slips away from him and quickly boxes his ears. He stops.*]

TAYLOR.

That was a darned silly thing to do.

NORAH.

What did you expect?

TAYLOR.

I expected you was cleverer than to hit me. You see, when it comes to—to muscle, I guess I've got the bulge on you.

NORAH.

I'm not frightened of you.

TAYLOR.

Now come and wash up these things.

NORAH.

I won't.

TAYLOR.

Come on.

[*He takes her wrists and tries to drag her to the table. She struggles with him, but cannot release herself. She kicks him as he drags her to the table.*]

NORAH.

Let me go.

TAYLOR.

Come on now, my girl. What's the good of making a darned fuss about it?

NORAH.

You brute, how dare you touch me! You'll never force me to do anything. Let go! Let go! Let go!

[*As they reach the table she bends down and bites him. Instinctively he releases her.*]

TAYLOR.

Gee, what sharp teeth you've got.

NORAH.

You cad! You cad!

TAYLOR.

[*Looking at his hand.*] I never thought you'd bite. That ain't much like a lady.

NORAH.

You filthy cad to hit a woman.

TAYLOR.

Gee, I didn't hit you. You smacked my face and kicked my shins, and you bit my hand. And then you say *I* hit you.

NORAH.

[*With all her passion.*] You beast! I hate you.

TAYLOR.

I don't care about that so long as you wash them cups.

NORAH.

Look.

[*With a sudden sweep of the arm she brushes them off the table, and they fall on the floor and break.*]

TAYLOR.

That's a pity. We're terribly short of crockery. We shall have to drink our tea out of tins now.

NORAH.

I said I wouldn't wash them and I haven't washed them.

TAYLOR.

They don't need it now, I guess.

NORAH.

I think I've won.

TAYLOR.

[*With a smile.*] Sure. Now take the broom and sweep up all the darned mess you've made.

NORAH.

I won't.

TAYLOR.

Look here, my girl, I guess I've had about enough of your nonsense. You do as you're told and look sharp about it.

NORAH.

You can kill me if you like.

TAYLOR.

What's the good of that? Women are scarce in Manitoba.... Here's the broom.

NORAH.

If you want that mess swept up you can sweep it up yourself.

TAYLOR.

You make me tired. [*He puts the broom into her hands, but she flings it violently away.*] Look here, if you don't clean up that mess at once, I'll give you the biggest hiding you've ever had in your life.

NORAH.

[*Scornfully.*] You?

TAYLOR.

[*Nodding his head.*] Yours truly. I've done with larking now.

[*He turns up the sleeves of his sweater. Suddenly she bursts into loud cries.*]

NORAH.

Help! Help! Help!

TAYLOR.

What's the good of that? There ain't no one within a mile of us. Listen.

[*For a moment they are both silent as they listen to the silence of the prairie.*]

NORAH.

If you touch me I'll have you up for cruelty. There are laws to protect me.

TAYLOR.

I don't care a curse for the laws. I know I'm going to be master here. And if I tell you to do a thing you've darned well got to do it because I can make you. Now stop fooling. Pick up that crockery and get the broom.

NORAH.

I won't.

[*He strides up and is just about to catch hold of her when she shrinks back. She sees he is in earnest. She is terrified by his look.*]

NORAH.

No, don't. Don't hurt me.

TAYLOR.

[*He stops and looks at her.*] I guess there's only one law here, and that's the law of the strongest. I don't know nothing about cities. Perhaps men and women are equal there. But on the prairie a man's master because he's bigger and stronger than a woman.

NORAH.

Frank.

TAYLOR.

Blast you, don't talk!

[NORAH *pauses, struggling between her pride and her fear. She will not look at her husband. She feels that he is getting impatient. At last, slowly, she bends down and picks up the teapot, the cups and saucers, and puts them on the table. Then she sinks into the chair and bursts into tears. He watches her with a slight smile on his face, but not unkindly.*]

NORAH.

Oh, I'm so unhappy.

TAYLOR.

[*Without any anger in his voice.*] Come on, my girl, don't shirk the rest of
it.

[*She looks up and sees the mess of spilt tea on the floor. She gets up slowly, keeping her face
away from him, and picks up the broom. She sweeps up. When she has finished she puts
the broom in the corner. He watches her all the time. Then she takes up her hat and coat
and starts to put them on.*]

TAYLOR.

What are you doing?

NORAH.

I've done what you made me do. Now I'm going.

TAYLOR.

Where?

NORAH.

What do I care so long as I get away?

TAYLOR.

You ain't under the impression that there's a first-class hotel round
the corner, are you? because there ain't.

NORAH.

I'll go to the Sharps.

TAYLOR.

I guess they're in bed and asleep by now.

NORAH.

I can wake them.

TAYLOR.

You'd never find your way. It's pitch dark.

NORAH.

I'll sleep out of doors, then.

TAYLOR.

On the prairie? Why, you'd freeze to death.

NORAH.

What does it matter to you whether I live or die?

TAYLOR.

It matters a great deal. Women are scarce in Manitoba.

NORAH.

Are you going to prevent me from going?

TAYLOR.

Sure.

[*He stands in front of the door and faces her.*]

NORAH.

You can't keep me here against my will. If I don't go to-night, I can go to-morrow.

TAYLOR.

To-morrow's a long way off.

[*She gives a start and looks at him with staring, terrified eyes, her throat is dry with terror.*]

NORAH.

Frank. What d'you mean?

TAYLOR.

I don't know what silly fancies you had in your head. When I married you I intended that you should be a proper wife to me.

NORAH.

But ... but.... [*She can hardly speak.*] But you understood. [*He does not answer. At last she collects herself. She tries to talk calmly and reasonably.*] I'm sorry for the way I behaved, Frank. It was childish of me to struggle with you. You irritated me by the way you spoke.

TAYLOR.

Oh, I don't mind. I don't know much about women and I guess they're queer. We had to fix things up sometime and I guess there was no harm in getting it over right now.

NORAH.

You've beaten me all along the line and I'm in your power. Have mercy on me.

TAYLOR.

I guess you won't have much cause to complain.

NORAH.

I married you in a fit of temper. It was very stupid of me. I'm very sorry that I—that I've been all this trouble to you. Won't you let me go?

TAYLOR.

No, I can't do that.

NORAH.

I'm no good to you. You've told me that I'm useless. I can't do any of the things that you want a wife to do. You can't be so hard-hearted as to make me pay with all my life for one moment's madness.

TAYLOR.

What good would it do if I let you go? Will you go to Gertie and ask her to take you back again? You've got too much pride for that.

NORAH.

I don't think I've got much pride left.

TAYLOR.

Don't you think you'd better give it a try?

NORAH.

All the life was so strange to me. In England they think it's so different from what it really is. I thought I should have a horse to ride. I expected dances and tennis parties. And when I came out I was so out of it. I felt in the way. And yesterday they drove me frantic so that I felt I couldn't stay another moment in that house. It was only an impulse. I made a mistake. I didn't know what I was doing. You can't have the heart to take advantage of it.

TAYLOR.

I knew you was making a mistake, but that was your look out. When I sell a man a horse he can look it over for himself, but I ain't obliged to tell him its faults.

NORAH.

D'you mean to say that after I've begged you almost on my knees to let me go you'll force me to stay?

TAYLOR.

Sure.

NORAH.

Oh, I'm so unhappy.

TAYLOR.

Perhaps you won't be when you get used to it.

NORAH.

[*Desperately.*] Oh, why did I ever walk into this trap?

TAYLOR.

Come, my girl, let us let bygones be bygones and give me a kiss.

[*She looks at him for a moment.*]

NORAH.

I'm not in love with you.

TAYLOR.

I guessed that.

NORAH.

And you're not in love with me.

TAYLOR.

You're a woman and I'm a man.

NORAH.

D'you want me to tell you in so many words that you're physically repellent to me? The thought of letting you kiss me horrifies and disgusts me.

TAYLOR.

[*Good-humouredly.*] Thank you.

NORAH.

Look at your hands. It gives me goose-flesh when you touch me.

TAYLOR.

Cutting down trees, diggin', looking after horses, don't leave them very white and smooth.

NORAH.

Let me go. Let me go.

[TAYLOR *changes his manner, which has been quite good-humoured, and speaks more sharply and with a certain stern force.*]

TAYLOR.

See here, my girl—you was educated like a lady and spent your life doing nothing—a lady's companion, wasn't you—taking a little dawg out for a walk of a morning and combing out his pretty little coat? And you look upon yourself as a darned sight better than me. I never had no schooling, and it's a hell of a job for me to write a letter, but since I was so high I've earned my living. I guess I've been all over this country. I've been a trapper and I've worked on the railroad, and for two years I've been a freighter. I guess I've done pretty near everything but serve in a store. Now you just get busy and forget all the nonsense you've got in your head. You're nothing but an ignorant woman and I'm your master. I'm going to do what I like with you, and if you don't submit willingly, by God I'll take you as the trappers in the old days used to take the squaws.

[*He steps towards her, and she, escaping from him, seizes his gun, which is lying against the wall. She lifts it and aims at him.*]

NORAH.

If you move I'll kill you.

TAYLOR.

[*Stopping suddenly.*] You daren't.

NORAH.

Unless you open the door and let me go I'll shoot you. I'll shoot you.

TAYLOR.

[*Advancing one step.*] Shoot, then.

[*She pulls the trigger. A click is heard, but nothing more.*]

TAYLOR.

Gee whiz, you meant it.

NORAH.

[*Aghast.*] It wasn't loaded.

TAYLOR.

Of course it wasn't loaded. D'you think I'd have stood there and told you to shoot if it had been? I guess I ain't thinking of committing suicide.

NORAH.

And I almost admired you.

TAYLOR.

You hadn't got no reason to. There's nothing to admire about a man who stands five feet off a loaded gun that's being aimed at him. He's a darned fool, that's all.

NORAH.

[*Throwing the gun aside angrily.*] You were laughing at me. Now I'll never forgive you.

TAYLOR.

You'd have had me dead as mutton if that gun had been loaded. You're a sport. I never thought you had it in you.

NORAH.

I'll never forgive you.

TAYLOR.

You're the girl for me, I guess.

[*Before she is prepared he flings his arms round her and tries to kiss her. She struggles desperately, turning her face away from him.*]

NORAH.

Let me alone. I'll kill myself if you touch me.

TAYLOR.

I guess you won't.

[*He gives her a resounding kiss on the cheek and lets her go. Sinking into a chair, she puts her hands up to her flaming cheeks.*]

NORAH.

Oh, how shameful, how shameful.

[*She sobs in helpless, angry despair. He puts his hand gently on her shoulder.*]

TAYLOR.

Hadn't you better cave in, my girl? You've tried your strength against mine and it didn't amount to much. You tried to shoot me and I only made you look a darned fool. I guess you're beat, my girl. There's only one law here, and that's the law of the strongest. You've got to do what I want because I can make you.

- 88 -

NORAH.

Haven't you any generosity?

TAYLOR.

Not the kind you want, I guess.

NORAH.

Oh, I'm so unhappy.

TAYLOR.

Listen. [*He puts up his finger and seems to listen intently. She looks at him, but does not speak.*] Listen to the silence. Can't you hear it, the silence of the prairie? Why, we might be the only two people in the world, you and me, here in this shack right out in the prairie. Listen. There ain't a sound. It might be the garden of Eden. What's that about male and female created He them? I guess you're my wife, my girl, and I want you. [*She gives him a sidelong look of terror, but still does not speak. He takes the lamp and goes to the bedroom door. He opens it and, holding the lamp up high, looks at her. Just to do something she takes the dishcloth and rubs the table with it. She wants to gain time.*] I guess it's getting late. You'll be able to have a good clean out to-morrow.

NORAH.

To-morrow.

[*A look of shame, fear, anguish, passes over her face, and then, violently, a convulsive shudder runs through her whole body. She puts her hands to her eyes and walks slowly to the door.*]

END OF THE THIRD ACT

ACT IV

SCENE: *The same as in the previous act,* FRANK TAYLOR'S *shack at Prentice, but there are signs about it of a woman's presence. There is a cloth on the table, and a cushion on the rocking-chair, there are muslin curtains on the window tied back with ribband, and there are geraniums growing in maple-syrup tins. There is a rough bookshelf against the wall, on which is* NORAH'S *small stock of books. Coloured supplements from the Christmas numbers of illustrated papers are pinned neatly on the walls. The packing-cases which had been used as stools have been replaced by rough chairs which* TAYLOR *has made with his own hands during the winter. When the door of the shack is opened the blue sky is seen and the prairie.* NORAH *is arranging mustard flowers in a pudding basin on the table. She wears a serge skirt and a neat shirt-waist: she has a healthier look than before, her face is tanned and she has a higher colour. She hears a sound and looks up.* TAYLOR *enters.*

NORAH.

I didn't know you were about.

TAYLOR.

I ain't got much to do to-day. I've been out with Sid Sharp and a man come over from Prentice.

NORAH.

Oh!

TAYLOR.

[*Noticing the flowers.*] Say, what have you got there?

NORAH.

Aren't they pretty? I picked them just now. They're so cheerful.

TAYLOR.

[*Drily.*] Very.

NORAH.

A few flowers make the shack look so much more bright and cosy.

TAYLOR.

[*Looking round him.*] You've made it a real home, Norah. Mrs. Sharp never stops wondering how you done it. Sid was saying only the other day it was because you was a lady. It does make a difference, I guess.

NORAH.

[*With a little smile.*] I'm glad you haven't found me quite a hopeless failure.

TAYLOR.

I guess I've never been so comfortable in all my life. It's what I always said—when English girls do take to the life they make a better job of it than anybody.

NORAH.

What's the man come out from Prentice for?

TAYLOR.

[*After a moment's pause.*] I guess you ain't been terribly happy here, my girl.

NORAH.

What on earth makes you say that?

TAYLOR.

You've got a good memory, I guess, and you ain't ever forgiven me for that first night.

NORAH.

[*Looking down.*] I made up my mind very soon that I must accept the consequences of what I'd done. I tried to fall in with your ways.

TAYLOR.

You was clever enough to see that I meant to be master in my own house, and I had the strength to do it.

NORAH.

[*With a faint smile.*] I've cooked for you and mended your clothes, and I've kept the shack clean. I've been obedient and obliging.

TAYLOR.

[*With a little chuckle.*] I guess you hated me sometimes.

NORAH.

No one likes being humiliated as you humiliated me.

TAYLOR.

Ed's coming out here presently, my girl.

NORAH.

Ed who?

TAYLOR.

Your brother.

NORAH.

[*Astounded.*] Eddie? When?

TAYLOR.

Why, right now, I guess. He was in Prentice this morning.

NORAH.

How d'you know?

TAYLOR.

He phoned over to Sharp's to say he was riding out.

NORAH.

Oh, how ripping! Why didn't you tell me before?

TAYLOR.

I didn't know.

NORAH.

Is that why you asked me if I was happy? I couldn't make out what was the matter with you.

TAYLOR.

Well, I guess I thought if you still wanted to quit, Ed's coming would be kind of useful.

NORAH.

Why d'you think I want to?

TAYLOR.

You ain't been very talkative these months, but I guess it wasn't hard to see you'd have given pretty near anything in the world to quit.

NORAH.

I'm not going back to Eddie's farm, if that's what you mean.

TAYLOR.

If he comes before I get back, tell him I won't be long. I guess you won't be sorry to do a bit of yarning with him by yourself.

NORAH.

You're not under the impression I'm going to say beastly things about you to him?

TAYLOR.

No, I guess not. That ain't your sort. P'raps we don't know the best of one another yet, but I reckon we know the worst by now.

NORAH.

[*Looking at him sharply.*] Frank, is anything the matter?

TAYLOR.

Why, no. Why?

NORAH.

You've seemed different the last few days.

TAYLOR.

I guess that's only your fancy. I'd better be getting along. Sid and the other fellow are waiting for me.

[*He goes out.* NORAH *looks at him with a puzzled air, then she gives a touch to the flowers, and gets her work. She sits down at the table and begins to mend a thick woollen sock. Suddenly there is a loud knock at the door. She starts up and runs to open it.* EDWARD MARSH *is seen standing outside. She gives a cry of delight and flings her arms round his neck. He comes in.*]

NORAH.

Eddie! Oh, my dear, I'm so glad to see you.

MARSH.

Hulloa there!

NORAH.

But how did you come? I never heard a rig.

MARSH.

Look.

[*She goes to the door and looks out.*]

NORAH.

- 93 -

Why, it's Reggie Hornby. [*Calling.*] Reggie.

HORNBY.

[*Outside.*] Hulloa!

NORAH.

He can put the horse in the lean-to.

MARSH.

Yes. [*Calling.*] Reg, give the old lady a feed and put her in the lean-to.

HORNBY.

Right-o.

NORAH.

Didn't you see Frank? He's only just this moment gone out.

MARSH.

No.

NORAH.

He'll be in presently. Now, come in. Oh, my dear, it is splendid to see you.

MARSH.

You're looking fine, Norah.

NORAH.

Have you had dinner?

MARSH.

Sure. We got something to eat before we left Prentice.

NORAH.

Well, I'll make you a cup of tea.

MARSH.

No, I won't have anything, thanks.

NORAH.

You're not a real Canadian yet if you refuse a cup of tea when it's offered you. Well, sit down and make yourself comfortable.

MARSH.

How are you getting on, Norah?

NORAH.

Oh, never mind about me. Tell me about yourself. How's Gertie? And what brought you to this part of the world? And what's Reggie Hornby doing? And is thingamygig still with you? You know, the hired man. What was his name? Trotter, wasn't it? Oh, my dear, don't sit there like a stuffed pig, but speak to me, or I shall shake you.

MARSH.

My dear, I can't answer fifteen questions all at once.

NORAH.

Oh, Eddie, I'm so glad to see you. You are a duck to come and see me.

MARSH.

Let me get a word in edgeways.

NORAH.

I won't say another syllable. But for goodness' sake, hurry up. I want to know all sorts of things.

MARSH.

Well, the first thing is that I'm expecting to be a happy father in three or four months.

NORAH.

Oh, Eddie, I'm so glad. How happy Gertie must be!

MARSH.

She doesn't know what to make of it. But I guess she's pleased right enough. She sends you her love and says she hopes you'll follow her example soon.

NORAH.

I? But you've not told me what you're doing in this part of the world, anyway.

MARSH.

[*Smiling.*] Anyway?

NORAH.

[*With a laugh.*] I've practically spoken to no one but Frank for months. I get into his ways of speaking.

MARSH.

Well, when I got Frank's letter about the clearing machine....

NORAH.

[*Interrupting him.*] Has Frank written to you?

MARSH.

Why, yes. Didn't you know? He said there was a clearing machine going cheap at Prentice. I've always thought I could make money down our way if I had one. They say you can clear from three to four acres a day with it. Frank said it was worth my while coming to have a look at it, and he guessed you'd be glad to see me.

NORAH.

How funny of him not to say anything to me about it.

MARSH.

I expect he wanted to surprise you. Now, how d'you like being a married woman?

NORAH.

Oh, all right. Why has Reggie Hornby come with you?

MARSH.

D'you know, I've not seen you since you were married.

NORAH.

You haven't, have you?

MARSH.

I've been a bit anxious about you. That's why, when Frank wrote about the clearing machine, I didn't stop to think about it, but just came.

NORAH.

It was very nice of you. But why has Reggie Hornby come?

MARSH.

Oh, he's going back to England.

NORAH.

Is he?

- 96 -

MARSH.

Yes, he got them to send him his passage at last. His ship doesn't sail till next week, and he said he might just as well stop off here and say good-bye to you.

NORAH.

How has he been getting on?

MARSH.

What do you expect? He looks upon work as something that only damned fools do. Where's Frank?

NORAH.

Oh, he's out with Sid Sharp. That's our neighbour. He has the farm you passed on your way here.

MARSH.

Getting on all right with him, Norah?

NORAH.

Of course. What's that boy doing all this time? He *is* slow, isn't he?

MARSH.

It's a great change for you, this, after the sort of life you've been used to.

NORAH.

[*To change the topic.*] I was rather hoping you'd have some letters for me. I haven't had any for a long time.

MARSH.

There now, I've got a head like a sieve. Two came by the last mail and I didn't send them on because I was coming myself.

NORAH.

You haven't forgotten them?

MARSH.

No, here they are.

NORAH.

[*Reading the addresses.*] They don't look very exciting. One's from Agnes Pringle. She was a lady's companion that I used to know in Tunbridge Wells. And the other's from Mr. Wynne.

MARSH.

Who's he?

NORAH.

Oh, he was Miss Wickham's solicitor. He wrote to me once before to say he hoped I was getting on all right. [*Putting the letters on the table.*] I don't think I want to hear from people in England any more.

MARSH.

My dear, why d'you say that?

NORAH.

It's no good thinking of the past, is it?

MARSH.

Aren't you going to read your letters?

NORAH.

Not now. I'll read them when I'm alone.

MARSH.

Don't mind me.

NORAH.

It's so silly of me, but letters from England always make me cry.

MARSH.

[*Looking at her sharply.*] Norah, aren't you happy here?

NORAH.

Yes, why shouldn't I be?

MARSH.

Why haven't you written to me once since you were married?

NORAH.

I hadn't got much to say. [*With a smile.*] And after all, I'd been practically turned out of your house.

MARSH.

[*Puzzled.*] I don't know what to make of you.

NORAH.

[*Nervous and almost exasperated.*] Oh, don't cross-examine me, there's a dear.

MARSH.

Frank Taylor's kind to you and all that sort of thing, isn't he?

NORAH.

Quite.

MARSH.

When I asked you to come and stay on the farm I thought it wouldn't be long before you married, but I didn't expect you'd marry one of the hired men.

NORAH.

Oh, my dear, don't worry about me.

MARSH.

It's all very fine to say that. You've got no one in the world belonging to you but me, and when—when our mother died, she said: "You'll take care of Norah, won't you, Eddie?"

NORAH.

[*With a sob in her voice.*] Oh, don't, don't.

MARSH.

Norah.

NORAH.

[*With an effort at self-possession.*] We've never quarrelled since the first day I came here. Here's Reggie.

[*She turns to him with relief.* HORNBY *is dressed in a blue serge suit and again looks like a well-groomed English gentleman.*]

NORAH.

[*Gaily.*] I was wondering what on earth you were doing with yourself.

HORNBY.

[*Shaking hands with her.*] I say, this is a very swell shack you've got.

NORAH.

- 99 -

I've tried to make it look pretty and homelike.

[MARSH *catches sight of the bowl of mustard flowers.*]

MARSH.

Hulloa, what's this?

NORAH.

Aren't they pretty? I've only just picked them. Mustard flowers.

MARSH.

We call it weed. Have you got much of it?

NORAH.

Oh yes, lots. Why?

MARSH.

Oh, nothing.

NORAH.

[*To* HORNBY.] I hear you're going home.

HORNBY.

Yes, I'm fed up with God's own country. Nature never intended me to be an agricultural labourer.

NORAH.

What are you going to do now?

HORNBY.

[*With immense conviction.*] Loaf!

NORAH.

[*Amused.*] Won't you get bored?

HORNBY.

I'm never bored. It amuses me to look at other people do things. I should hate my fellow creatures to be idle.

NORAH.

[*With a faint smile.*] I should have thought one could do more with life than lounge about clubs and play cards with people who don't play as well as oneself.

HORNBY.

I quite agree with you. I've been thinking things over very seriously this winter. And I'm going to look out for a middle-aged widow with money who'll adopt me.

NORAH.

I remember that you have decided views about the White Man's Burden.

HORNBY.

All I want is to get through life comfortably. I don't mean to do a stroke more work than I'm obliged to, and I'm going to have the very best time I can get.

NORAH.

[*Smiling.*] I'm sure you will.

HORNBY.

The moment I get back to London I'm going to stand myself a slap-up dinner at the Ritz, then I shall go and see a musical comedy at the Gaiety, and after that I'll have a slap-up supper at Romano's. England, with all thy faults, I love thee well.

NORAH.

I suppose it's being alone with the prairie all these months, things which used to seem rather funny and clever—well, I see them quite differently now.

HORNBY.

[*Coolly.*] I'm afraid you don't altogether approve of me.

NORAH.

[*Not disagreeably.*] You haven't got pluck.

HORNBY.

I don't know about that. I expect I have as much as anyone else, only I don't make a fuss about it.

NORAH.

Oh, pluck to stand up and let yourself be shot at—I daresay. But pluck to do the same monotonous thing day after day, plain, honest, hard work—you haven't got that. You're a failure, and the worst of it is, you're not ashamed of it. It fills you with self-satisfaction.

HORNBY.

Rule Britannia, and what price the Union Jack?

NORAH.

[*With a laugh.*] You're incorrigible.

HORNBY.

I am.... I suppose there's nothing you want me to take home. I shall be going down to Tunbridge Wells to see mother. Got any messages?

NORAH.

I don't know that I have. Eddie has just brought me a couple of letters. I'll have a look at them. [*She opens Miss Pringle's letter, reads two or three lines, and gives a cry.*] Oh!

MARSH.

What's the matter?

NORAH.

What does she mean? [*Reading.*] "I've just heard from Mr. Wynne about your good luck, and I have another piece of good news for you." [*She puts the letter down and quickly opens the solicitor's. She takes out of the envelope a letter and a cheque. She glances at it.*] A cheque—for five hundred pounds.... Oh, Eddie, listen. [*Reading.*] "Dear Miss Marsh,—I have had several interviews with Mr. Wickham in relation to the late Miss Wickham's estate, and I ventured to represent to him that you had been very badly treated. Now that everything is settled he wishes to send you the enclosed cheque as some recognition of your devoted service to his late aunt...." Five hundred pounds!

MARSH.

That's a very respectable sum.

HORNBY.

I could do with that myself.

NORAH.

I've never had so much money in all my life.

MARSH.

But what's the other piece of good news that Miss Stick-in-the-mud talks about?

NORAH.

- 102 -

Oh, I forgot. [*She takes Miss Pringle's letter up again and begins to read it.*] "...Piece of good news for you. I write at once so that you may make your plans accordingly. I told you in my last letter of my sister-in-law's sudden death, and now my brother is very anxious that I should live with him. So I am leaving Mrs. Hubbard, and she wishes me to say that if you care to have my place as her companion she will be very pleased to have you. I have been with her for thirteen years, and she has always treated me like an equal. She is very considerate, and there is practically nothing to do but to exercise the dogs. The salary is thirty-five pounds a year."

MARSH.

Both letters are addressed to Miss Marsh. Don't they know you're married?

NORAH.

No. I never told them.

HORNBY.

What a lark! You could go back to Tunbridge Wells, and none of the old frumps would ever know you'd been married.

[NORAH *gives a sudden start when he says this and stares at him with wide-open eyes. There is a moment's pause.*]

MARSH.

Just clear out for a minute, Reg. I want to speak to Norah.

HORNBY.

Right-o.

[*He goes out.*]

MARSH.

Norah, d'you want to clear out?

NORAH.

What on earth makes you think that?

MARSH.

You gave him such a look when he mentioned it.

NORAH.

I'm bewildered. Did Frank know anything about this?

MARSH.

My dear, how could he?

NORAH.

It's so extraordinary. He was talking about my going away just now.

MARSH.

[*Quickly.*] Why?

NORAH.

Oh!

[*She realises that she has betrayed the secret inadvertently.*]

MARSH.

Norah, for goodness' sake tell me if there's anything the matter. After all, it's now or never. You're keeping back something from me. Aren't you getting on well together?

NORAH.

[*In a low voice.*] Not very.

MARSH.

Why didn't you let me know?

NORAH.

I was ashamed.

MARSH.

But you say he's kind to you.

NORAH.

I've got nothing to reproach him with.

MARSH.

I felt that something was wrong. I knew you couldn't be happy with him. A girl like you and a hired man. The whole thing was horrible. Thank God I'm here and you've got this chance.

NORAH.

What d'you mean?

MARSH.

You're not fit for this life. You've got a chance to go back to England. For God's sake take it. In six months all you've gone through here will seem nothing but a hideous dream. [*He is suddenly struck by the expression of her face.*] Norah, what's the matter?

NORAH.

[*Tragically.*] I don't know.

[HORNBY *comes in again.*]

HORNBY.

I say, here's someone coming to see you.

NORAH.

Me? [*She goes to the door and looks out.*] Oh, it's Mrs. Sharp. Whatever brings her here on foot? She never walks a step if she can help it. She's the wife of my neighbour.... Good-afternoon, Mrs. Sharp.

[MRS. SHARP *enters. She is a middle-aged woman, red in the face, stout and rather short of breath. She wears an old sun-bonnet, a faded shirt-waist, none too clean, and a rather battered skirt.*]

NORAH.

Come right in.

MRS. SHARP.

Good-afternoon to you, Mrs. Taylor. I'm all in a perspiration. I've not walked so far in months.

NORAH.

This is my brother.

MRS. SHARP.

Your brother? Is that who it is?

NORAH.

[*Smiling.*] It seems to surprise you.

MRS. SHARP.

I was so anxious, I couldn't stay indoors. I went out to see if I could catch sight of Sid, and I walked on and then I saw the rig what's outside, and it give me such a turn, I thought it was the inspector. I just had to come. I was that nervous.

NORAH.

Is anything the matter?

MRS. SHARP.

You're not going to tell me you don't know about it? Why, Sid and Frank haven't been talking about anything else since Frank found it.

NORAH.

Found what?

MRS. SHARP.

The weed.

MARSH.

[*With a slight gesture towards the pudding bowl of flowers.*] You have got it, then?

MRS. SHARP.

It's worse at Taylor's. But we've got it too.

NORAH.

What does it mean?

MRS. SHARP.

We can't make out who reported us. It isn't as if we had any enemies.

MARSH.

Oh, there's always someone to report you. No one's going to take the risk of letting it get on his own land.

MRS. SHARP.

[*Looking at the mustard blossom.*] And she has them in the house as if they were flowers.

NORAH.

Tell me what she means, Eddie.

MARSH.

My dear, these pretty little flowers which you've picked to make your shack look bright and homelike—they may mean ruin.

NORAH.

Eddie!

MARSH.

You must have heard us talk about the weed. We farmers have three enemies to fight—frost, hail, and weed.

MRS. SHARP.

We was hailed out last year. Lost our crop. We never got a dollar for it. And if we lose it this year too—why, we may just as well quit.

MARSH.

When it gets into your crop you've got to report it, and if you don't one of the neighbours will. And then they send an inspector along, and if he condemns it, why you just have to destroy the crop, and all your year's work is lost. You're lucky if you've got a bit of money in the bank and can go on till the next crop comes along.

MRS. SHARP.

We've only got a quarter section and five children. It's not much money you can save then.

MARSH.

Are they out with the inspector now?

MRS. SHARP.

Yes. He came out from Prentice this morning.

MARSH.

This is a bad job for Frank.

MRS. SHARP.

Oh, he hasn't got the mouths to feed that we have. He can hire out again. But what's to become of us?

NORAH.

I wonder why he never told me.

MRS. SHARP.

I guess he's in the habit of keeping his troubles to himself and you've not taught him different yet.

[NORAH *gives her a quick look, but seeing the woman is all on edge with nervousness does not answer.*]

MARSH.

You must hope for the best, Mrs. Sharp.

- 107 -

MRS. SHARP.

Sid says we've only got it in one place, but perhaps he's only saying it so I shouldn't worry. You know what them inspectors are. They don't lose nothing by it. It don't matter to them if you starve all the winter.

[*She gives a sob and heavy tears roll down her cheeks.*]

NORAH.

Oh don't—don't cry, Mrs. Sharp. After all, it may be all right.

MARSH.

They won't condemn the crop unless it's very bad. Too many people have got their eyes on it. The machine agent, the loan company.

MRS. SHARP.

What with the hail that comes and hails you out and the frost that kills your crop just when you're beginning to count on it, and the weed—I can't bear it any more. If we lose this crop I won't go on. I'll make Sid sell out and we'll go home. We'll take a little shop somewhere. That's what I wanted to do from the beginning, but Sid—he had his heart set on farming.

NORAH.

You couldn't go back now. You'd never be happy in a little shop. And if you'd stayed in England you'd have been always at the beck and call of somebody else. And you own the land. You couldn't do that in England. When you come out of your door and look at the growing wheat, aren't you proud to think it's yours?

MRS. SHARP.

You don't know what I've had to put up with. When the children came, only once I had a doctor. The other times Sid was the only help I had. I might have been an animal. I wish I'd never come to this country.

NORAH.

How can you say that! Your children are strong and healthy. Why, they'll be able to help you in the work soon. You've given them a chance that they'd never have got at home.

MRS. SHARP.

Oh, it's all very well for them. They'll have it easy. I know that. But we've had to pay for it, Sid and me.

NORAH.

You see, you were the first. It's bitter work opening up a new country and perhaps it's others who reap the harvest. But I wonder if those who start don't get a reward that the later comers never dream of.

MARSH.

She's right there, Mrs. Sharp. I shall never forget what I felt when I saw my first crop spring up and thought that never since the world began had wheat grown on that little bit of ground.... I wouldn't go back to England now for anything in the world. I couldn't breathe.

MRS. SHARP.

You're a man. You have the best of it and all the credit.

NORAH.

People don't know. You mustn't blame them. It's only those who've lived out on the prairie who know that the hardships of opening up a new country fall on the women. But the men who are their husbands, they know.

MARSH.

I guess they do, Mrs. Sharp.

[NORAH, *on her knees beside her, strokes* MRS. SHARP'S *hands.* MRS. SHARP *gives her a grateful smile.*]

MRS. SHARP.

Thank you for speaking kindly to me, my dear. I'm that nervous, I hardly know what I'm saying.

NORAH.

Sid and Frank will be here in a minute, surely.

MRS. SHARP.

And you're right, my dear, I couldn't go back any more. If we lose our crop, well, we must wait till next year. We shan't starve. One's got to take the rough with the smooth, and take it all in all, it's a good country.

[FRANK TAYLOR *comes in.*]

NORAH.

Frank.

MRS. SHARP.

[*Starting to her feet.*] Where's Sid?

TAYLOR.

Why he's up at your place. Hulloa, Ed. I saw you coming along in the rig. Morning, Reg. I wasn't expecting to see you.

HORNBY.

Pleasant surprise for you.

MRS. SHARP.

What's happened? Tell me what's happened.

NORAH.

Mrs. Sharp came here because she was so anxious.

TAYLOR.

[*Cheerfully.*] Oh, you're all right.

MRS. SHARP.

[*With a gasp.*] We are?

TAYLOR.

Sure. Only a few acres has got to go. That won't hurt you.

MRS. SHARP.

Thank God for that. And it's going to be the best crop we ever had. It's the finest country in the world.

TAYLOR.

You'd better be getting back. Sid's taken the inspector up to give him some dinner.

MRS. SHARP.

He hasn't? That's just like Sid. It's a mercy there's plenty. I'll be getting along right now.

NORAH.

Don't walk. There's Eddie's rig. Reggie will drive you over.

MRS. SHARP.

Oh, thank you kindly. I'm not used to walking so much and I'm tired out. Good-afternoon, Mrs. Taylor.

NORAH.

Good-bye. Reggie, you don't mind driving Mrs. Sharp back? It's only just over a mile.

HORNBY.

Not a bit.

MARSH.

I'll come and help you put the mare in.

[MRS. SHARP *and* HORNBY *go out.*]

MARSH.

I guess it's a relief to you now you know, Frank.

TAYLOR.

Terrible.... I'd like to have a talk with you presently, Ed.

MARSH.

Right you are. [*He goes.*]

NORAH.

I'm so thankful it's all right. Poor thing, she was in such a state.

TAYLOR.

They've got five children to feed. I guess it makes a powerful lot of difference to them.

NORAH.

I wish you'd told me before. I felt that something was worrying you and I didn't know what.

TAYLOR.

If I saved the crop there didn't seem any use fussing, and if I didn't you'd know quite soon enough.

NORAH.

How could you bear to let me put the flowers here?

TAYLOR.

I guess I didn't mind if it made you happy. You didn't know they was only a weed. You thought them darned pretty.

NORAH.

[*With a little smile.*] It was very kind of you, Frank.

- 111 -

TAYLOR.

I guess it's queer that a darned little flower like that should be able to do so much damage.

NORAH.

Why didn't you tell me you'd written to Eddie?

TAYLOR.

I guess I forgot.

NORAH.

Frank, Eddie brought me some letters from home to-day. I've had the offer of a job in England.

[FRANK *is just going to make an exclamation, but immediately controls himself and answers quite quietly.*]

TAYLOR.

Gee! I guess you'll take that.

NORAH.

It's funny that you should have been talking just now of my going away.

TAYLOR.

Very.

NORAH.

[*A little surprised at his manner.*] Have you any objection?

TAYLOR.

I guess it wouldn't make a powerful lot of difference to you if I had.

NORAH.

What makes you think that?

TAYLOR.

I guess you only stayed here because you had to.

[*She goes over to the little window and looks out at the prairie.*]

NORAH.

Is life always like that? The things you've wanted so dreadfully seem only to bring you pain when they come. [*He gives her a quick look, but does not*

- 112 -

answer, and she notices nothing.] Month after month I used to sit looking at the prairie and sometimes I wanted to scream at the top of my voice just to break the silence. I thought I should never escape. The shack was like a prison. I was hemmed in by the snow and the cold and the stillness.

TAYLOR.

Are you going to quit right now with Ed?

NORAH.

[*With a smile.*] You seem in a great hurry to be rid of me.

TAYLOR.

I guess we ain't made a great success of married life, my girl.... It's rum when you come to figure it out. I thought I could make you do everything I wanted. It looked as if I held a straight flush. And you beat me.

NORAH.

I?

TAYLOR.

Why, yes. Didn't you know that?

NORAH.

I don't know what you mean.

TAYLOR.

I guess I didn't know how strong a woman could be. You was always givin' way, you done everything I told you—and all the time you was keepin' something from me that I couldn't get at. Whenever I thought to put my hand on you, I guess I found I'd only caught hold of a shadow.

NORAH.

I don't know what more you wanted.

TAYLOR.

I guess I wanted love.

NORAH.

You?

[*She looks at him with consternation. His words give her a queer little twist of the heart-strings.*]

TAYLOR.

I know you now less than when you'd only been a week up at Ed's. I've lost the trail and I'm just floundering around in the bush.

NORAH.

[*In a low voice.*] I never knew you wanted love.

TAYLOR.

I guess I didn't either.

NORAH.

I suppose parting's always rather painful.

TAYLOR.

If you go back to the Old Country, I guess—I guess you'll never come back.

NORAH.

[*Rather shyly.*] Perhaps you'll come over to England one of these days. If you have a couple of good years you could easily shut the place up and run over for the winter.

TAYLOR.

I guess that would be a dangerous experiment. You'll be a lady in England, and I guess I'd be just the hired man.

NORAH.

You'd be my husband.

TAYLOR.

I guess I wouldn't risk it.

NORAH.

You'll write to me now and then and tell me how you're getting on, won't you?

TAYLOR.

Will you want to know?

NORAH.

[*Smiling.*] Why, yes.

TAYLOR.

I'll write and tell you if I'm making good. If I ain't, I guess I shan't feel much like writing.

NORAH.

But you'll make good, Frank. I know you well enough for that.

TAYLOR.

Do you?

NORAH.

I have learnt to respect you during these months we've lived together. All sorts of qualities which I used to value seem very unimportant to me now. You've taught me a great deal.

TAYLOR.

You'll think of me sometimes, my girl, won't you?

NORAH.

[*Smiling.*] I don't suppose I shall be able to prevent it.

TAYLOR.

I was an ignorant, uneducated man. I didn't know how to treat you properly. I wanted to make you happy and I didn't seem to know just how to do it.

NORAH.

You've never been unkind to me, Frank. You've been very patient with me.

TAYLOR.

I guess you'll be happier away from me. I'll be able to think that you're warm and comfortable at home and you've got plenty to eat.

NORAH.

D'you think that's all I want?

[*He gives her a rapid glance, and then setting his teeth looks away.*]

TAYLOR.

I couldn't expect you to stay on here, not when you got a chance of going back to the Old Country. This life is all new to you. And you know that one.

NORAH.

Oh, yes, I know it—I should think I did. [*As she pictures to herself the daily round which awaits her, she is filled with a sort of mirthless scorn, and this presently, as she speaks, is mixed with hatred and dismay.*] At eight o'clock every morning a maid will bring me tea and hot water. And I shall get up, and I shall have breakfast, and I shall interview the cook. I shall order luncheon and dinner. And I shall brush the coats of Mrs. Hubbard's poms and take them for a walk on the common. All the paths on the common are asphalted so that elderly gentlemen and lady's companions shouldn't get their feet wet.

TAYLOR.

Gee!

NORAH.

And then I shall come in and lunch, and after luncheon I shall go for a drive, one day in this direction and one day in that. And then I shall have tea, and then I shall go out again on the nice neat asphalt paths to give the dogs another walk. And then I shall change my dress and come down to dinner. And after dinner I shall play bezique with my employer, and I must take care not to beat her because she doesn't like being beaten. And at ten o'clock I shall go to bed.... [*She pauses a moment.*] At eight o'clock next morning a maid will bring in my tea and hot water, and the day will begin again. Every day will be just like every other. And there are hundreds of women in England, strong and capable, with blood in their veins, who would be eager to get the place that's offered to me. Almost a lady and thirty-five pounds a year.

[TAYLOR *has been gazing at her steadily. What she means begins to dawn on him, but he restrains himself. He will not look at her now.*]

TAYLOR.

I guess it's a bit different from the life you've had here.

NORAH.

[*Turning to him.*] And you will be clearing the scrub, cutting down trees, ploughing the land, sowing and reaping. You will be fighting every day, frost, hail, and weed; you will be fighting, but I know you'll be conquering in the end. Where was wilderness will be cultivated land. And who knows what starving child may eat the bread that has been made from the wheat that you grew. My life will be ineffectual and useless, but you will have done something worth while.

TAYLOR.

Why, what's the matter with you, Norah, Norah?

[*He does not say the words to her, but rather to himself as though they were forced from him in agony of spirit.*]

NORAH.

When I was talking to Mrs. Sharp just now I don't know what I said, I was just trying to comfort her because she was crying, and it seemed to be someone else who was speaking, and I listened to myself. I thought I hated the prairie through the long winter months, and yet somehow it has caught hold of me. It was dreary and monotonous, and yet I can't get it out of my heart. There's a beauty and a romance in it which fill my soul with longing.

TAYLOR.

[*Quietly.*] I guess we all hate the prairie sometimes, but when you've once lived in it, it ain't easy to live anywhere else.

NORAH.

I know the life now. It's not adventurous and exciting. For men and women it's the same hard work from morning till night, and I know it's the women who bear the greater burden. The men go into the towns, they have shooting now and then, and the different seasons bring them different work. But for the women it's always the same, cooking, mending, washing, sweeping. And yet it's all got a meaning. We, too, have our part in opening up the country. We are its mothers and the future is in us. We are building up the greatness of the nation. It needs our courage and strength and hope, and because it needs them, they come to us. Oh, Frank, I can't go back to that petty, narrow life. What have you done to me?

TAYLOR.

[*Hoarsely.*] I guess if I asked you to stay now, you'd stay.

NORAH.

[*In a low voice.*] You said you wanted my love. Don't you know?... Love has been growing in me slowly, month by month, and I wouldn't see it. I told myself I hated you. I was ashamed. It's only to-day, when I had the means of leaving you for ever, that I knew I couldn't live without you. I'm not ashamed any more. I love you.

TAYLOR.

I guess I loved you from the beginning, Norah.

NORAH.

Why d'you say it as if...? What's the matter, Frank?

TAYLOR.

I guess you'll have to take that job in England. I can't ask you to stay on.

NORAH.

Why?

TAYLOR.

The inspector's condemned the crop. I'm bust.

NORAH.

Oh, why didn't you tell me?

TAYLOR.

I guess I couldn't. I made up my mind when I married you that I'd make good. I couldn't expect you to see that it was just bad luck. Anyone can get the weed in his crop. But I guess a man oughtn't to have bad luck. The odds are that it's his own fault if he has.

NORAH.

Now I understand about Eddie.

TAYLOR.

I wrote to him when I knew I'd been reported.

NORAH.

What are you going to do?

TAYLOR.

It's all right for me. I can hire out. It's you I was thinking of. I felt pretty sure you wouldn't go back to Ed's. I didn't fancy you taking a position as lady help. I didn't know what was to become of you, my girl. And when you told me of the job in England, I thought I'd let you go.

NORAH.

Without telling me you were in trouble?

TAYLOR.

Why, if I wasn't smashed up, d'you think I'd let you go? By God, I wouldn't. I'd have kep' you—by God, I'd have kep' you.

NORAH.

Are you going to give the land up?

TAYLOR.

No, I guess I can't do that. I've put too much work in it. And I've got my back up now. I shall hire out for the summer and next winter I can get work lumbering. The land's my own now, and I'll come back in time for the ploughing next year.

NORAH.

Look.

TAYLOR.

What's that?

[*She hands him the cheque which she has received from Mr. Wynne.*]

NORAH.

The nephew of the lady I was with has made me a present of it. Twenty-five hundred dollars. You can lake the quarter section next to this one and get all the machinery you want and some cows. It's yours to do what you like with. Now will you keep me?

TAYLOR.

Oh, my girl, how shall I ever be able to thank you!

NORAH.

Good heavens, I don't want thanks. There's nothing in the world so wonderful as to be able to give to someone you love.... Give me a kiss and try.

TAYLOR.

I guess it's the first time you've asked me to do that.

NORAH.

Oh, I'm so happy.

THE END

CPSIA information can be obtained
at www.ICGtesting.com
Printed in the USA
BVHW081726111022
649158BV00008B/1112